Genetic Engineering

by Tina Kafka

LUCENT BOOKS
A part of Gale, Cengage Learning

GALE
CENGAGE Learning

Detroit • New York • San Francisco • New Haven, Conn • Waterville, Maine • London

LIBRARY OF CONGRESS CATALOGING-IN-PUBLICATION DATA

Kafka, Tina, 1950–
   Genetic engineering / by Tina Kafka.
      p. cm. -- (Hot topics)
   Includes bibliographical references and index.
   ISBN 978-1-4205-0148-3 (hardcover)
   1. Genetic engineering--Juvenile literature. I. Title.
   QH442.K332 2009
   174'.957--dc22

2009005288

Lucent Books
27500 Drake Rd.
Farmington Hills, MI 48331

ISBN-13: 978-1-4205-0148-3
ISBN-10: 1-4205-0148-8

Dedication
This book is dedicated to the generosity of Freeman J. Dyson and others who are willing to share their knowledge and to explain abstract concepts in science and history to a curious English literature major.

Printed in the United States of America
1 2 3 4 5 6 7 13 12 11 10 09

CONTENTS

FOREWORD

Young people today are bombarded with information. Aside from traditional sources such as newspapers, television, and the radio, they are inundated with a nearly continuous stream of data from electronic media. They send and receive e-mails and instant messages, read and write online "blogs," participate in chat rooms and forums, and surf the Web for hours. This trend is likely to continue. As Patricia Senn Breivik, the former dean of university libraries at Wayne State University in Detroit, has stated, "Information overload will only increase in the future. By 2020, for example, the available body of information is expected to double every 73 days! How will these students find the information they need in this coming tidal wave of information?"

Ironically, this overabundance of information can actually impede efforts to understand complex issues. Whether the topic is abortion, the death penalty, gay rights, or obesity, the deluge of fact and opinion that floods the print and electronic media is overwhelming. The news media report the results of polls and studies that contradict one another. Cable news shows, talk radio programs, and newspaper editorials promote narrow viewpoints and omit facts that challenge their own political biases. The World Wide Web is an electronic minefield where legitimate scholars compete with the postings of ordinary citizens who may or may not be well-informed or capable of reasoned argument. At times, strongly worded testimonials and opinion pieces both in print and electronic media are presented as factual accounts.

Conflicting quotes and statistics can confuse even the most diligent researchers. A good example of this is the question of whether or not the death penalty deters crime. For instance, one study found that murders decreased by nearly one-third when the death penalty was reinstated in New York in 1995. Death penalty supporters cite this finding to support their argument that the existence of the death penalty deters criminals from committing murder. However, another study found that states without the death penalty have murder rates below the national average. This study is cited by opponents of capital punishment, who reject the claim that the death penalty deters murder. Students need context and clear, informed discussion if they are to think critically and make informed decisions.

The Hot Topics series is designed to help young people wade through the glut of fact, opinion, and rhetoric so that they can think critically about controversial issues. Only by reading and thinking critically will they be able to formulate a viewpoint that is not simply the parroted views of others. Each volume of the series focuses on one of today's most pressing social issues and provides a balanced overview of the topic. Carefully crafted narrative, fully documented primary and secondary source quotes, informative sidebars, and study questions all provide excellent starting points for research and discussion. Full-color photographs and charts enhance all volumes in the series. With its many useful features, the Hot Topics series is a valuable resource for young people struggling to understand the pressing issues of the modern era.

INTRODUCTION

A Scientific Revolution

As the first decade of the twenty-first century draws to a close, most scientists agree that science is in the throes of one of the greatest revolutions since Galileo invented the telescope six hundred years ago. Galileo's invention changed accepted ideas about Earth's place in the universe. Once they could see beyond Earth's horizon, scientists began to understand that Earth is only a tiny fraction of a universe whose boundaries are still unknown. These ideas were not readily accepted, however. In fact, Galileo was rejected by his church and exiled from his home for his belief that the sun, not Earth, was the center of the solar system.

In a similar way, the field of genetic engineering is changing scientists' understanding of life itself. Boundaries that have been taken for granted are now questioned. When genes from one species can be combined with those from another, doubt is placed on the concept of a species as a unique group of genetic traits. Even the difference between plants and animals becomes blurred when genes from a fish, for instance, are engineered into a tomato in order to breed a tomato that is resistant to cold. Is the resulting organism an animal or a plant?

Unanswered Questions

Many profound questions arise along with this rapidly growing science. Scientists and others argue about how to draw the line between ethical and unethical research, whether genetic engineering research should be limited, and who decides. Scientists, politicians, and various interest groups debate the safety of genetically modified foods and how much risk is tolerable in the search for solutions to urgent health problems. But even as debate rages, biologists continue to move forward and focus with increasing scrutiny on the most basic mechanisms of life. And, as they continue to finely tune their focus, the power of genetic engineers to manipulate those mechanisms grows mightier.

The foundation of genetic engineering, like that of all science, is built upon past achievements. In the 1950s scientists James Watson and Francis Crick described the double helix structure of the DNA molecule, which contains coded instructions that direct the structure and function of every part of every living organism. They explained that the DNA molecule is shaped like a twisted ladder. Each rung of that ladder is a joined pair of chemicals called bases. The pairs are composed of either adenine and thymine (A-T or T-A), or guanine and cytosine (G-C or C-G). Every living organism—plant or animal—contains these same four bases arranged in pairs along strands of sugar and phosphate. A gene is a specific sequence, or pattern, of these chemical pairs. Differences between individuals and even between species lie solely in the sequence of these chemicals along the strand.

However, many view the work of two scientists in the 1970s, Herb Boyer and Stanley Cohen, as the most direct link between past research and modern genetic engineering. Boyer and Cohen found a way to cut DNA apart and recombine the parts in new ways. The general term for the resulting molecule is recombinant DNA.

Shortly after, scientists found they could transfer genes from animals and plants into bacteria. The bacteria, in turn, would then work like tiny factories churning out large quantities of the hormones or other chemicals directed by the transplanted gene. In 2004 the two scientists won the prestigious Albany Medical Center Prize in Medicine and Biomedical Research for this research that set the stage for modern genetic engineering.

It is usually difficult to gauge the enormity of a scientific advance at the time it is taking place. No one predicted, for example, that the discovery of the structure of the DNA molecule would change the criminal justice system. Nor did computer scientists foresee in the 1970s that computers would shrink dramatically in size, that teenagers would create social networks online, or that vast amounts of information would be available at no cost to anyone with access to a computer small enough to fit on a person's lap.

In the same way, the applications of genetic engineering are just beginning to reveal themselves. The implications of the ability to recombine DNA from different species and direct organisms to produce medicines, chemicals, organs for human transplant, and new foods appear as limitless as the human imagination. Scientists are learning to identify sequences along the DNA molecule responsible for certain diseases such as diabetes, Alzheimer's, Parkinson's, cancer, and heart disease, among others. They are searching for key sequences responsible for outstanding qualities such as musical talent or athletic ability. Once these sequences are identified, scientists will gain the ability to add or subtract them at will.

New Name for an Old Science

Though the science of genetics is relatively new, even the first farmers learned to save the seeds each year from the fattest barley, the tastiest corn, and the most productive wheat. They sowed those seeds the following year in the hope of improving their harvest. Over time, crops changed to reflect the tastes of the farmers and those they fed. Domesticated animals followed a similar path. The tastiest hogs, the most productive cows, and the best chickens, among others, were bred selectively to improve the stock. Robert Krulwich, a science writer for National Public Radio, explained on a segment for *Morning Edition* in 2008 how genetic engineering has changed over time: "Humans have been doing this for centuries, of course, using the breeding techniques that have produced Chihuahuas and poodles, and different varieties of apples and bananas, but bioengineering, tinkering with the DNA, produces those changes much more quickly."[1]

An article in the *New York Times* published in June 1987—a little more than twenty years ago—illustrates Krulwich's point. The article outlines some possible future scenarios in the rising field of modern genetic engineering. At the time, these ideas seemed like science fiction: plants that could produce their own pesticides and weed killers, the ability to select the gender of animals by manipulating the cells that produce eggs and sperm, the transfer of genes from one species to another, the birth of cloned mammals, and the ability of an animal of one species to gestate and give birth to an animal of a different species.

Not only have these scenarios been realized, they now seem almost commonplace. In the 1990s corn and cotton were genetically modified to produce their own pesticides. In 1996 Dolly, a sheep cloned from the udder cell of another sheep, was born in Scotland. In 2001 Bessie the cow gave birth to Noah, the gaur, an endangered Asian ox. Scientists have genetically modified rice to contain high amounts of vitamin A by transferring daffodil and bacteria genes into the rice's genome. Pets, including dogs, cats, and even a bull, have been cloned. Pigs, implanted with human genes, grow organs for human transplant that will not be rejected by their recipients. The gene responsible for spiderweb silk has been engineered into goats.

Genetically engineered pigs can grow organs that are transferrable to human recipients without being rejected.

Genetic engineering is already forging new paths in more directions and more quickly than anyone ever imagined. Bioengineers are developing computer programs that read the sequence of an individual's genetic makeup, or genome, quickly. In 2003 the first full human genome sequence was completed. The Human Genome Project, as it was known, took thirteen years and cost $437 million to complete. By 2008 the time needed to read a human genome was reduced to four weeks and cost one-hundred thousand dollars. Some scientists predict that by 2015, new parents will pay ten dollars to have their baby's DNA sequence read at birth and placed in his or her medical file. This information will enable doctors both to predict the likelihood that the baby is prone to a disease and to interfere genetically with the disease before it strikes.

The knowledge that entire organisms are just various arrangements of a limited number of chemicals has fueled an entirely new field of genetic engineering called biosynthesis, "BioSyn" a process that is, in effect, the reverse of reading a genome's sequence. Instead of reading an existing genome, scientists use the basic ingredients to build an entirely new organism from scratch. This, of course, raises many new questions. Is a life form just a machine made of parts strung together, each of which has a specific function? Some bioengineers think so. This is another issue with which society must grapple as the science of genetic engineering moves steadily forward.

PHARMING: THE DISEASE OR THE CURE?

People have relied on plants and parts of animals to make medicine for thousands of years. Some native species, in fact, still form the basis of modern drug therapies. Digitalis, a substance found in foxglove, a common plant that grows in modern gardens, is the basis of many heart medicines. Modern surgeons use curare, a by-product of plants from South America, to relax a patient's muscles during surgery. Morphine, a potent painkiller, is produced from a common wildflower, the opium poppy. Even penicillin, used to treat many infections, is the natural product of a mold.

Though medicines made from plants and even animal parts are not new, until now each species of medicinal plant or animal part has been kept separate. In the 1920s, for example, scientists discovered that insulin, a hormone produced in the pancreas, is needed to process sugar in the body. Diabetics, people whose bodies no longer make insulin, fell ill and often died as the effects of high levels of sugar in their blood took their toll. Since animal insulin is almost identical genetically to human insulin, drug companies soon began producing pharmaceutical insulin from the readily available pancreases of slaughtered cows and pigs. Though the lives of many diabetics were saved, some diabetics developed allergies to this nonhuman insulin. But as the techniques of recombining DNA were perfected, researchers were able to engineer the human insulin gene into bacteria. The bacteria then became tiny factories able to produce vast amounts of human insulin. This eliminated the allergy problem. These advances were important, but they were only the beginning.

Once genetic engineers learned to cut and recombine genes, the possibilities of developing drugs to treat human diseases and even organs for human transplant became almost limitless. At the beginning of the twenty-first century, genetic engineering is still in its infancy. But already, the magnitude of the possible medical applications of this new technology is apparent. Freeman J. Dyson, a physicist on the faculty of the Institute for Advanced Studies in Princeton, New Jersey, speaks and writes frequently about the future of new technology. In his book *The Sun, the Genome, and the Internet*, he refers to the future of genetic engineering when he says, "The medical scientists of today will be leading revolutions into directions that we can only dimly discern."[2] Dyson is not alone at expressing awe at what may be possible when drug therapies are no longer limited by the genomes of individual species.

A BOON FOR ALL

"Genetically modified animals should be a boon both for consumers, who may ultimately gain healthier foods and access to scarce medications, and for agricultural producers, who may cut costs with disease-resistant or faster-growing animals." —*New York Times* editorial.

New York Times, "Coming to a Plate Near You," editorial, October 3, 2008. www.nytimes.com/2008/10/04/opinion/04sat3.html.

After Dolly Came Polly

Shortly after the celebrated birth of Dolly the cloned sheep in Scotland in 1996, Ian Wilmut, the scientist who cloned Dolly, used the same process to clone Polly, another sheep. This time, however, Wilmut added a human gene to the sheep cell during the cloning process. His goal was to develop a treatment for hemophilia, a genetic disorder in which people lack the protein that helps blood to thicken and clot after an injury. People afflicted with hemophilia risk bleeding to death, even from minor bumps and bruises.

When Polly matured, her milk contained the lifesaving human clotting protein missing in hemophiliacs. Hemophiliacs who drink the milk from the genetically engineered sheep are then able to form blood clots. Wilmut envisioned creating herds of genetically engineered sheep to treat this disorder. Polly, however, represented more than the hope for a cure for one more disease. The fledgling biotech industry—propelled by advances in genetic engineering—was taking flight.

While the blood of hemophiliacs does not form blood clots, another blood disorder results in blood that thickens and clots too much. Victims of this disorder are susceptible to heart attacks and strokes. A small biotechnology company in Massachusetts, GTC Biotherapeutics, is genetically engineering goats in order to

Cloned sheep Dolly (right) and Polly (left). Polly's milk contains the lifesaving human clotting protein missing in hemophiliacs, so when people with the disorder consume it, they are then able to form blood clots.

develop a drug called ATryn to find a cure for this deadly disorder. ATryn is produced when "pharmers"—scientists who develop pharmaceuticals—engineer a human gene that produces antithrombin, the protein that prevents clotting, into newly fertilized goat embryos.

An article titled "Pharm Animals Crank Out Drugs," published in the online journal Wired, explains the purpose of the fourteen hundred goats that graze on GTC Biotherapeutics' rolling Massachusetts farmland: "The animals are sophisticated drug incubators, with millions of dollars of potential profit accumulating in their udders each day."[3] When the genetically engineered female goats mature, their milk contains the protein antithrombin, which is then purified into a form that can be administered to humans.

In the past, tiny amounts of this protein could be gathered only from human blood donations, a process that is inefficient and expensive. GTC foresees raising herds of genetically engineered goats to supply patients with ample antithrombin and GTC stockholders with healthy profits. Each goat produces 2.2 pounds (1kg) of antithrombin each year, while blood donations from fifty thousand people are required to produce the same amount.

Chickens That Lay Golden Eggs

Goats are not the only farm animals finding human genes in their DNA. Scottish biologist Helen Sang is incubating a plan to produce chicken eggs enhanced with proteins for treating a variety of human diseases. Since the whites, or albumin, of chicken eggs already contain high concentrations of protein, fortifying chicken eggs with human proteins seems a natural extension. Chickens, like rabbits, reproduce quickly. Also, of course, each chicken lays many eggs, creating a potential gold mine for the biotech firm that devises a system for creating custom eggs on demand to fill prescriptions for specific diseases.

Scientists at Origen Therapeutics, a biotech firm in northern California, are also working with chickens to develop eggs that produce human proteins. Scientists there hope eventually to breed chickens with eggs capable of producing the entire range of human antibodies to treat many diseases that afflict mankind. Elizabeth Svoboda, science writer for Wired, explains how this accomplishment might ease the process of producing medicines: "If the company succeeds, harvesting compounds for drug therapies will be a little like choosing a flavor from a soda fountain."[4] Given the lightning-fast progress of this technology in the last several years, this advance may be on the near horizon.

Causing Diseases with Genetic Engineering

While many researchers work on enhancing the milk, blood, and eggs of animals to provide ready supplies of human medicines, other scientists perform genetic modifications to deliberately induce certain diseases in animals. In this way, scientists study exactly what goes wrong on the genetic level when humans develop certain diseases. In England, for example, rhesus monkeys are genetically engineered to develop Huntington's disease, a devastating progressive illness that results in uncontrolled tremors, memory loss, personality changes, and ultimately, death.

UNFAIR TO ANIMALS

"Genetic engineering is responsible for a skyrocketing increase in the numbers of animals being used in laboratory experiments and is likely to have drastic long term ill effects in the animals themselves." —Catherine Willett, science policy adviser for People for the Ethical Treatment of Animals.

Quoted in Elizabeth Svoboda, "Pharm Animals Crank Out Drugs," Wired, February 14, 2007. www.wired.com/medtech/health/news/2007/02/72708.

Animal rights activists, however, condemn using animals in this way to benefit humans. While acknowledging that medical research is important, Maggie Jennings, a spokesperson for the Royal Society of the Prevention of Cruelty to Animals in England, said, "There are many different ways of carrying out research on these diseases without using primates. The animal suffering involved, in our view is considerable."[5]

Anthony Chan, who led the study on the monkeys, counters that it would be unethical *not* to use every possible means to find a cure for this debilitating illness. The gene responsible for this disease was discovered in 1993, but so far scientists have been unable to find a way to reverse the brain deterioration that results in the disease's devastating symptoms. Huntington's disease is particularly problematic, as it usually does not become evident until midlife. By then many victims of this disease have already had children. Each child of a Huntington's victim then has a fifty-fifty chance of developing the disease.

Monkeys in a lab are engineered to develop Huntington's disease to enable scientists to study the gene that causes it. They hope to determine whether it may be possible to reverse the devastating brain deterioration caused by the disease.

Genetic engineering may also help solve the riddle of why apparently healthy infants sometimes die during their first year of life. Sudden infant death syndrome (SIDS) is an unexpected tragedy that kills more than two thousand American babies each year. Until now, doctors could only advise worried parents to protect their babies by not smoking and by placing sleeping infants on their backs." In July 2008 the prestigious scientific journal *Science* published a report suggesting that SIDS deaths might be the result of an imbalance in a brain chemical called serotonin.

An Italian research team stumbled on the connection between low levels of serotonin and SIDS when they genetically engineered mice to reduce serotonin levels. To their surprise, more than half of the genetically engineered mice died suddenly before they were three months old. Scientists, however, note that the cellular systems in mice and humans are not identical. They are not yet certain that the SIDS-serotonin connection applies to human babies.

Pigs That Glow

While many scientists who research human diseases use animals in their studies, animal rights advocates object to manipulating and sacrificing the lives of animals to benefit human medical research. Scientists at National Taiwan University in 2006, for example, successfully transferred the fluorescent green protein from jellyfish into cloned pig embryos. The internal organs of the resulting piglets then glowed green under ultraviolet light. Moreover, the little pigs also sported green tint around their ears, eyes, and snouts. The study team was gratified when the glow trait was passed from one of the genetically altered pigs to two of its little piggy babies.

This proved two points: The pig with the jellyfish gene was fertile, and the altered gene could be inherited. This genetic engineering feat could prove important to stem cell research and to the search for a way to monitor the health of tissue in organ transplants while it heals. Tissue that glows is easy to track under ultraviolet light. According to Science Buzz, the online Science Museum of Minnesota, "At last report, the mother pig was doing fine and glowing with pride."[6] This development may speed the

Glowing with Pride

In October 2008 three scientists learned they had been awarded the Nobel Prize in Chemistry for work with the genes that cause jellyfish to glow. Osamu Shimomura, Martin Chalfie, and Roger Y. Tsien shared the honors. Biologists have known for a long time that some jellyfish glow in the dark. When the gene responsible for the glowing protein, dubbed GFP for "green fluorescent protein," was identified in the early 1990s, Chalfie engineered it into six cells of a transparent roundworm he was studying and found that the six cells glowed like tiny lanterns. Tsien later developed ways to mutate the gene to create a palette of colorful proteins, including yellow, blue, cyan, and orange. Scott LaFee, science writer for the *San Diego Union-Tribune*, explains the importance of this research: "The benefits of this work can be counted in the tens of thousands of experiments and investigations that have been done and are being done using fluorescent proteins—everything from probes of basic cellular functions to understanding the biologies of cancer and Alzheimer's disease to developing new drugs and medical therapies." The GFP gene has even been incorporated into a work of art. In 2000 artist Eduardo Kac commissioned a French laboratory to genetically engineer a rabbit with the GFP gene. The result: Alba, a green, glowing, baby bunny.

Scott LaFee, "Shining Examples," *San Diego Union-Tribune*, October 16, 2008, p. E4.

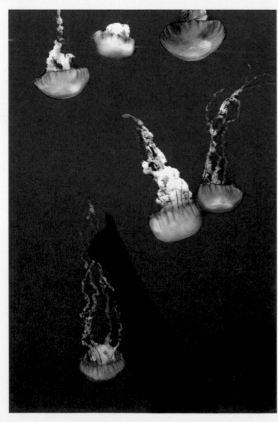

The gene that causes some jellyfish to glow is called GFP. A French laboratory genetically engineered a rabbit with GFP, causing it to glow.

production of pigs bred specifically to grow organs for human transplant. The glowing organs would enable doctors to monitor the health of the transplanted organs without subjecting their human recipients to invasive surgical procedures. The donor pigs, however, would still sacrifice their organs.

Animal rights activists object to animals dying for the sake of human medical research. They also object to any animal experimentation at all. As computer simulations of animal systems become more available, an outspoken group voices the view that any laboratory research on animals, including manipulating their genetic makeup, is cruel and unnecessary. In response to such criticism, many medical schools and universities have eliminated the use of live animals in research studies. Others counter, however, that a computer simulation cannot substitute for the observation of live animals.

Cures on the Cob

Animals can lay genetically engineered eggs, give genetically engineered milk, and grow genetically engineered organs, but genetically engineering animals is expensive and labor intensive. Each animal needs space to live and requires expensive ongoing care. It is more practical and cost efficient to raise genetically engineered vegetables than it is to genetically engineer the DNA of animals. Many biotechnology companies, in fact, stake their futures on their ability to genetically engineer grain crops to produce medicines that benefit human health.

A small biotechnology company in San Diego, California, is one such company. Epicyte Pharmaceuticals pioneered the technique of genetically engineering corn to produce a drug to treat the herpes simplex virus, which causes painful sores sometimes known as "cold sores" around the lips, mouth, and face. Epicyte also gained fame in the early 2000s for genetically engineering corn so that men who ate cereals or other products made from the corn became sterile and could not father children.

However, unlike animals, in which breeding can be carefully monitored, corn pollen spreads with the breeze, which makes it difficult to control. In fact, the growing biotech industry suffered a major setback in 2000, when genetically engineered corn intended for animal feed was discovered in Taco Bell taco shells sold in grocery stores. Known as Starlink corn, the grain was genetically engineered to contain bacteria that make it toxic to the corn borer, a pest that feeds on growing corn. In effect, the corn produces its own insecticide.

Since the engineered corn was not approved for human consumption, Kraft Foods was forced to recall more than 2.5 million boxes of Taco Bell taco shells. The following year, farmers were not allowed to plant corn seed they had already purchased, since its purity could not be ensured. This incident, frequently referred to as "taco terrorism" or the "Starlink scandal," is often used to highlight the dangers of cross-contamination between fields of growing crops.

Despite concerns about contamination of food crops, many biotechnology companies are moving forward to genetically engineer corn, as well as other grains, to create pharmaceuticals. In Iowa, one farmer in 2002 grew a field of corn that was genetically engineered to produce a drug to treat cystic fibrosis. Victims of cystic fibrosis have difficulty breathing and often die young. ProdiGene, a biotech company based in College Station, Texas, is working to develop a strain of corn to function as an oral vaccine against the AIDS virus. While many applaud this technology, others fear contamination of nearby food crops. Critics point out that once pollen is released into the air, it cannot be recalled. Larry Bohlen, director of health and environment programs at Friends of the Earth, represents many who fear that "just one mistake by a biotech company and we'll be eating other people's prescription drugs in our corn flakes."[7]

Rice: Take One Teaspoon and Call Me in the Morning

Possible contamination of the food supply was also the major objection raised in 2007 when Ventria Bioscience in California gained approval from the federal government to plant genetically engineered rice in Kansas. Ventria's rice is engineered to produce two proteins normally found in breast milk. The proteins help children recover more quickly from diarrhea, one of the leading killers of young children worldwide. Kansas governor Kathleen Sebelius as

A woman and her infant leave a children's hospital in Peru. Several children in the country had allergic reactions to the genetically engineered rice that was thought to cure infant diarrhea.

well as the farmers who plan to grow this select—and lucrative— variety of rice applauded the decision by the U.S. Department of Agriculture's Animal Plant and Health Inspection Service. However, many individuals object to planting this crop in the nation's heartland—the farming regions of the country.

Critics of the government decision point to several cases of food supply contamination by GE (genetically engineered) crops, including one instance in 2002 when 500,000 bushels (17.6 million L) of soybeans in Nebraska and 155 acres (63ha) of corn in neighboring Iowa were contaminated by corn genetically engineered to contain a vaccine for pig diarrhea. The soybeans are used in many products, including baby food and ice cream. Prodigene, a leading biotech firm, was fined $250,000 and had to pay almost $3 million to compensate farmers in that case. In 2006 GE rice was found three times in rice intended for human consumption, which cost farmers

Nothing to Sneeze At!

Four thousand dollars can buy a no-sneeze kitten from Allerca, a small California biotech company that has genetically engineered a strain of felines that will not make human eyes itch and noses run. Though the price may seem steep, allergy sufferers who love cats have lined up to bring an Allerca kitten home. Prospective owners undergo a rigorous approval process to qualify for a hypoallergenic kitty. They are evaluated for motivation and warmth and questioned about how they will discipline their pet if it has an accident. People see the Allerca cats as the ideal way to resolve conflicts that arise in homes where cat lovers meet allergy sufferers. An article in the *New York Times*

outlines the issue: "That combination has made many homes cauldrons of sneezing, itchy conflicts in which a fiancé is allergic to his beloved's favorite pet, or a mother-in-law cannot come for a festive meal because of Fluffy's presence." Many cat owners spend thousands of dollars on medications, air filters, and other forms of relief rather than forego the comfort of a furry, purring friend. A no-sneeze kitty may well be worth its cost.

Elisabeth Rosenthal, "Cat Lovers Lining Up for No-Sneeze Kitties," *New York Times*, October 6, 2006. www .nytimes.com/2006/10/06/science/06cat.html?ex=13177 87200&en=b9d3e400389a522e&ei=5088&partner=rss nyt&emc=rss.

millions of dollars in export sales. European and Asian markets are especially wary of GE products.

Moreover, Ventria was highly criticized for bypassing the strict rules in the United States that govern drug trials on humans. Ventria conducted experiments on infants in rural Peru, and when some babies there had allergic reactions to the protein from GE rice, parents claimed they were not fully informed about the risks to their children. However, Kansas agriculture secretary Adrian Polansky voiced support for Ventria's program: "This is an important development for Kansas farmers, who stand to benefit from the additional income. They also have the satisfaction of knowing they are helping provide affordable healthcare products to children who desperately need it."[8] The tension between opposing interests continues to play out.

Keeping the Gene(ie) on the Pharm

Those who believe genetic engineering offers hope for both treatments and profits conflict on many fronts with those who resist this new technology. Containment is perhaps the most commonly cited issue. Many critics point to the difficulty of containing genetically engineered crops to keep them out of the food supply. Farmers have tried various strategies, some more successful than others. One method used by some of the largest biotech firms entails growing genetically engineered crops in isolated parts of Arizona, California, and Washington. By avoiding the Midwest, where farms are more plentiful, they hope to increase the physical distance between food crops and GE crops, making cross-pollination less likely. However, politicians from the Midwest are not enthusiastic about outlawing biopharms in their states altogether, as profits from those farms can be significant. Furthermore, environmental groups do not consider increasing the distance between crops a workable solution. A coalition of eleven environmental groups filed a lawsuit against the U.S. Department of Agriculture in 2003, hoping to ban the use of food crops for pharmaceutical use and restrict the plants to greenhouses. At the time, François Arcand, president of the Conference on Plant-Made Pharmaceuticals held that year in Quebec, said, "Molecular farming represents the pharmaceutical industry's best opportunity to strike a serious blow against such global diseases as AIDS, Alzheimer's and cancer."[9] A spokesperson for Monsanto, a biotech industry giant, concurred, warning that restricting biopharms to greenhouses would set the industry back by up to twenty years.

THE CONSTANT COMPANION OF PROGRESS: NOSTALGIA

"We tinker and change and endlessly imagine a more perfect future. And at the same time, we idealize the past, so we're trapped. Progress's constant companion is nostalgia for the way things used to be." —Ira Glass, host, *This American Life*.

Ira Glass, "In Iowa, No One Can Hear You Squeal," *This American Life,* Chicago Public Radio, April 26, 2007. www.thisamericanlife.org.

In an attempt to ward off criticism and ensure the isolation of "pharm" crops, a researcher from Purdue University in Indiana keeps his pharm underground. Controlled Pharming Ventures promotes underground cave pharming in an attempt to control the unintended spread of stray pollen. Doug Ausenbach, the company's founder, adapted a former limestone quarry and underground warehouse in Marengo, Indiana, to grow pharmaceutical corn, tobacco, soybeans, tomatoes, and potatoes. While growing crops in an environment that depends on artificial light and irrigation is more expensive, the increased expense is offset by higher yields per acre. The cave corn yielded 337 bushels per acre (29,346 L per ha), as opposed to 142 bushels per acre (12,365 L per ha) for conventional corn. In addition, the scientists are working on ways to recycle dead plants to provide energy to fuel the lighting system. Moreover, cave pharming may also work in tandem with the growing popularity of farming without pesticides, since common agricultural pests do not thrive underground.

However, critics point out that cave pharming is not enough to protect food crops from contamination. They remind the public

Cave pharming has become popular for several reasons, including the fact that pollen from genetically engineered crops cannot spread and contaminate other crops.

that shipping mishaps can also be blamed for contamination. The accidental mixing of Prodigene's vaccine-containing corn with Nebraska's soybeans is a prime example.

One Way to Guarantee Zero Contamination

Whether genetically engineered crops are restricted to caves, greenhouses, islands, or isolated farms, most people admit that it is impossible to guarantee with perfect certainty that pharm crops will not find their way into food crops. An article in *Scientific American* outlines the only possible way to ensure that they never mix: "Many researchers, as well as groups including the Union of Concerned Scientists, the Food Manufacturers of America and the Consumers Union, contend that the only measure sufficient to ensure zero contamination by pharmaceutical crops would be to avoid developing the technology in plants that can find their way into the stomachs of people or farm animals."[10]

However, the public, scientists, politicians, and interest groups on both sides of the issue agree that the technology has already advanced too far to turn back. The benefits and the dangers that accompany them pose a dilemma. Most of those involved agree that it is difficult, if not impossible, to reconcile two interests that are in direct conflict with each other: genetically engineering food crops for purposes other than food and guaranteeing that the food supply is safe from contamination.

Who Decides?

In the United States three government agencies regulate different aspects of the biotech industry. The U.S. Department of Agriculture (USDA) requires notification that tests will take place, issues permits to test certain varieties of plants that may be toxic, and then removes plants from further oversight once the tests are complete. The Food and Drug Administration (FDA) ensures that foods made from these plants are safe for humans and animals to eat. The Environmental Protection Agency (EPA) is responsible for the safety of pesticides. FDA publications claim that rigorous safety testing guidelines and consultation services help ensure safety. While acknowledging that consultation is voluntary, the FDA stands behind its policy, claiming, "Although consultation is voluntary on the part of developers, the legal requirements that the foods have to meet are not."[11] The FDA expresses confidence that biotech companies comply fully with the voluntary system.

GENES: YOU CANNOT LIVE WITH THEM, CANNOT LIVE WITHOUT THEM

"Genes make us sick or healthy, sane or crazy, fat or thin."—Freeman J. Dyson, physicist, Institute for Advanced Study, Princeton University.

Freeman J. Dyson, *The Sun, the Genome, and the Internet.* New York: Oxford University Press, 1999, p. 32.

Many consumer groups do not share the FDA's confidence. They point to a system that has no central authority and too many loopholes. Although decisions by these agencies are not supposed to be motivated by politics and pressure, they are vulnerable to both. Many believe the bottom line is not public interest but the interests of the biotech companies, whose future profits rest solely on decisions made by these agencies. Concerned scientists and members of the public insist the profit motive trumps safety. But pressure comes from all sides.

Pharmaceutical companies stand to profit when products are deemed effective and safe. Consumer groups insist that the effects of genetically modified products are still unknown. They fear that genetically engineered organisms (GEOs) will destroy the food supply and the environment and that once released, they cannot be recalled. Many countries are reluctant to import genetically engineered products, which gives decisions by U.S. government agencies power to affect the global economy. One thing is certain: While the growing field of pharming is ripe with controversy and passionate opinions, the technology of transferring genes back and forth between animals, humans, and plants to produce medicines continues to march steadily forward.

GENETICALLY ENGINEERED FOODS: WHOSE APPETITE DO THEY SATISFY?

While genetically engineering food crops to make medicines is highly controversial, changing the nutritional composition of food itself inflames the passions of both proponents and critics. Food inspires strong feelings because not only is it basic to survival, people associate the food they eat with nurture and comfort. Families hand favorite recipes down through the generations. As a result, when scientists begin to tinker with the basic composition of everyday foods, people react.

The Flavr Savr Cannot Be Saved

The first genetically engineered food hit the produce section of grocery stores in 1994. Calgene, a biotech company in California, began to market its Flavr Savr tomato. By transferring the information from a gene for antibiotic resistance into the tomato's genome, genetic engineers created a tomato that would not rot as quickly as a conventional tomato.

This solved a problem that long plagued tomato growers: In order to preserve the fruit (tomato is considered a fruit) and keep it fresh, farmers had to pick tomatoes while they were green and then chemically ripen them after shipping. Not only was chemical ripening distasteful to the public, the gas-ripened tomatoes lacked flavor. The Flavr Savr tomato, on the other hand, was hardier than the ordinary tomato. Farmers could allow it to ripen on the vine and ship it, and it would arrive in the supermarket still red, ripe, juicy, and ready to eat.

At the time, genetically engineered foods did not require special consideration from the Food and Drug Administration. However, before the Flavr Savr tomato hit the market after the 1993 growing season, the public raised alarms about its safety. To reassure the public, Calgene requested that the FDA issue a decision about the tomato's safety.

The following summer, the FDA ruled in favor of the Flavr Savr tomato, but as hardy as it was, Calgene and its tomato did

Genetic engineers created the Flavr Savr tomato by transferring the information from a gene for antibiotic resistance into the tomato's genome. The result was a tomato that would stay ripe for a longer period of time.

The Terminator

Named after a robotic killer played by California governor Arnold Schwarzenegger, the Terminator gene is genetically engineered into plant seeds. When these seeds ripen, molecular switches automatically turn off the seed's ability to reproduce. The seed can no longer sprout. The Terminator technology was first patented by Delta and Pine Land Company (D&PL), the world's largest cottonseed company, in 1998. No one paid much attention at the time, except Monsanto. Later that year Monsanto bought D&PL for $1.8 billion, making it the new owner of the Terminator patent. Monsanto now owns more than 20 percent of the world's seed. Owning this patent allows Monsanto to genetically engineer the Terminator gene into any of the seeds it sells. This scenario could devastate half of the world's farmers, who depend on the seeds from each year's harvest to plant the following year's crop. Once this gene is engineered into the seed they purchase, farmers must then purchase new seed for each planting season, an expense they cannot afford. Monsanto has announced plans to genetically engineer rice, soy, and wheat in the same way.

not last long. They both succumbed to competition from other biotech companies, a dip in prices, and a glut of GE tomatoes on the market. Eventually, Calgene sold a majority of its shares to Monsanto, another big biotech company.

Something Is Fishy About That Tomato

Though the Flavr Savr tomato beat it to market, the Flounder tomato is probably the more colorful character in the early history of genetically engineered foods. The effort to create tomatoes that could withstand cold was spearheaded by DNA Plant Technology Corporation. Scientists there engineered a gene from flounder, a fish that thrives in cold Arctic waters, into the DNA of tomatoes. The scientists hoped this gene transfer would create a tomato that could withstand frost in the field and resist cold damage in storage.

Though the experiment failed, the legend itself thrived. In fact, like many folk tales, this one has morphed. It turned into a story of strawberries with fish genes—appropriately named fishberries. In fact, according to the Public Issues Education Project of Cornell University, "There are no published studies involving strawberries, no companies which have announced research or marketing plans for such a product, no government records of field testing such a plant, and no trace in the media to explain how this story may have originated."[12] However, though fishberries may be imaginary, the legend still flourishes. It is often cited by critics to emphasize the foolishness of crossing natural genetic barriers.

Irreconcilable Differences

Although the first genetically engineered food to hit the grocery store aisles was a tomato, GE foods are actually far more common to other sections of the market. Flour, oil, salad dressings, pie, chips, cookies, fried foods, and candy coatings often contain genetically modified ingredients. In fact, a 2007 article in the *Los Angeles Times* reported, "largely unbeknownst to most consumers, more than 70 percent of processed foods on grocery store shelves contain genetically engineered or biotech ingredients."[13] The main sources, according to the article, are just three crops—corn,

More than half of the food in grocery stores contains genetically engineered ingredients.

soy, and canola—which are used in products to sweeten and thicken foods. Roughly 60 percent of the corn in the United States is engineered to contain a gene that comes from a bacterium called *Bacillus thuringiensis*, known as *Bt*. *Bt* is toxic to certain insects, including the European corn borer, corn's most destructive enemy. When the *Bt* gene is inserted into corn DNA, the corn produces its own pesticide. In other words, bug killer is built right into the plant.

Soybean farmers have also benefited from what is known as the first generation of genetically engineered foods. Nearly 90 percent of the U.S. soy crop is engineered with genes taken from bacteria that allow the plant to withstand sprayings of weed killers, such as Roundup, an herbicide often favored by soybean farmers. Soybean plants that have been genetically engineered in this way are often referred to as "Roundup Ready." Critics point to the alleged risk that these GE organisms represent to human health and the environment. Proponents of genetic engineering believe the risks are minimal and the potential for solving some of the world's most persistent problems such as hunger and malnourishment is great.

The Next Generation

Plants that produce their own bug killers and weed killers are only the beginning. Biotech companies and university labs are working on more complex genetic engineering feats to make crops that are richer in nutrients such as vitamins, minerals, and

Protecting Plants, Too

In April 2008 the Swiss federal government's ethics committee on nonhuman biotechnology issued guidelines that surprised, confused, and amused the scientific community. The guidelines require that all applications for plant research must include a paragraph that describes how the dignity of plants will be protected in the impending research.

omega-3 fatty acids. In some cases, scientists work to turn genes off so that plants will lack proteins that cause allergies.

At Alabama A&M University, for example, scientists are working to develop hypoallergenic peanuts. Scientists elsewhere are developing tomatoes that are richer in folic acid and potatoes that contain high levels of calcium. Monsanto is developing a soybean genetically altered to be lower in saturated fats and less prone to develop unhealthy trans fats when processed. At the University of California at Berkeley (UC Berkeley), Peggy Lemaux, a professor of plant and microbial biology, developed a variety of wheat that could be eaten by people with wheat allergies. Lemaux's recent research involves finding ways to increase genetically the nutritional value and digestibility of sorghum, a grain important to diets in Africa.

Supersize Fish in the Gene Pool

Scientists are also tinkering with the genes of foods other than grains in attempts to nourish the world's growing population. Research is well under way to genetically engineer both rainbow trout and salmon to grow bigger and meatier and to reach those sizes more quickly than conventional fish. The Agricultural Research Service, a government science agency, is working with private biotech companies to develop a variety of rainbow trout with an extra set of chromosomes. This extra set bestows two benefits onto the engineered trout. First, it ensures that the fish is sterile. These trout, therefore, cannot interbreed with wild trout, a criticism often leveled against genetically modified organisms (GMOs). Also, the sterile trout grow bigger and faster, since energy that would otherwise be expended in breeding is devoted only to growing. In the last several years, demand for larger fish in general has resulted in a market that favors bigger trout.

The trout's saltwater cousin the salmon has also been genetically engineered. Aqua Bounty Technologies in Massachusetts is hoping to gain FDA approval for a transgenic Atlantic salmon that has been engineered with two genes. The first is a growth hormone gene from the Chinook salmon, and the second is a gene from another fish—the ocean pout—that keeps the growth hormone flowing year-round. Ordinarily, salmon grow primarily during the warm summer months. This genetically engineered salmon, however, reaches market weight in only eighteen months, a full year ahead of conventional salmon.

The delay in bringing these big fish to the fish market stems from the difficulty in gaining approval from the FDA, the government agency that regulates food for human consumption. Elliot Entis, Aqua Bounty's chief executive, believes that the company has ensured the safety of the salmon. Moreover, he claims that Aqua Bounty has provided the FDA with evidence that the supersize salmon contains the same level of fats, proteins, and other nutrients and tastes the same as common farmed salmon. "Nobody has ever analyzed salmon as closely as we have done,"[14] Entis claims.

FDA approval is crucial, since the outcome of years of expensive research and the fortunes of biotech companies hinge on rulings by this government agency. Many farmers kept expensive cloned livestock for years before the FDA finally ruled in December 2006 that milk and meat from clones was safe to eat. And clones, which are genetic twins, do not contain genes from foreign organisms, further complicating an issue that is already emotional since it circumvents natural procreation.

GMOs: More Good than Harm?

"GMOs are going to be the best thing to happen to the American diet since pesticides. No, I'm not being snarky. Pesticides brought the cost of vegetables down dramatically; so many more people could afford them. I think we have to trust ourselves, and the next generations, to use the huge power of genetic engineering more-or-less wisely. Free consumers will choose better products; free voters will demand that government provide reasonable protections. It won't work perfectly (it hasn't so far), but it will do more good than harm. The world is speeding up; it's gonna be a great ride." —"lilnev," atheist-humanist, scientist.

Quoted in John Tierney, "Whole Foods v. Whole Earth," TierneyLab Blog, *New York Times,* March 3, 2007. http://tierneylab.blogs.nytimes.com/2007/02/26/whole-foods-v-whole-earth.

Aqua Bounty has engineered salmon with a growth hormone gene so the fish will be market-ready in only eighteen months, a full year ahead of conventional salmon.

Medium-Rare and Grown in a Vat

If the concept of genetically engineered corn and fish raises some hackles, the reaction is mild compared to the passions enflamed by some other foods. One day, slaughtering an animal may not be a prerequisite for consuming a steak or a chicken nugget. Some scientists are working to bypass the animal altogether and grow meat in vats. Morris Benjaminson, a biology professor at Touro College in New York, has extracted stem cells from fish embryos and chemically induced them to become muscle cells that look and taste like fish fillets. He foresees the day that chicken breasts will be mass-produced without the chickens and filet mignon produced without the steer.

A PRIME MINISTER WITH FORESIGHT

"Fifty years hence, we shall escape the absurdity of growing a whole chicken in order to eat the breast or wing, by growing these parts separately under a suitable medium." —Winston Churchill, former prime minister of England, 1936.

Quoted in Ben Macintyre, "Will the Petri Dish Put Daisy Out to Grass?" Times Online, January 13, 2007. http://business.timesonline.co.uk/tol/business/markets/europe/article1292346.ece?token=null&offset=0&page=1.

In Holland, Dutch researchers are conducting similar experiments with pig stem cells to produce vat-grown pork. Jason Metheny, a doctoral student at Johns Hopkins University, envisions a future in which meat is grown in sheets of fat and muscle cells. The advantage, according to Metheny: "In theory, with cultured meat, nothing is wasted, nothing suffers and nothing dies."[15] Metheny believes that consumers can be educated to accept vat-grown meat just as they now accept chickens and other livestock raised in what many consider less-than-ideal circumstances.

Chicken Things

If vegetarians avoid meat because they object to killing animals, vat-grown meat might increase the menu choices at vegetarian dinner tables. Animals will not even be involved in its production. Theoretically, once scientists perfect the technology of culturing meat from stem cells and genetically engineering it to contain less fat and more protein, very few cells are needed. In fact, Jack William Bell, a Seattle software engineer who writes about the future, suggests some gourmet possibilities: "Endangered species might no longer be taboo. What if we used cultures from endangered or even extinct species? Would it be okay to have Siberian tiger on a stick? Spotted owl nuggets? You could have that bowl of panda stew in good conscience."[16]

Animals naturally shed thousands of cells each day, so critics might be hard-pressed to argue that vat meat exploits animals. In fact, to the surprise of many, the powerful animal rights lobby People for the Ethical Treatment of Animals (PETA) announced in April 2008 that it would pay a million dollars to the first person to develop a practical method of producing edible meat without an animal by 2012.

The contest specifies that the product must look and taste like real chicken. The chickenlike product will be prepared using a fried chicken recipe and will be judged by a panel of ten PETA judges. The contest guidelines require that the company that submits the winning entry also prove that its product is practical to make and sell. They must produce at least 2000 pounds (970kg) and distribute it to fast-food restaurants and grocery stores in ten states over a period of three months. The cost must also mimic that of real chicken. Ingrid Newkirk, a founder of PETA, explained that the contest itself is controversial within the organization, since

Where's the Chicken?

People for the Ethical Treatment of Animals (PETA) has provoked quite an uproar within the organization by offering a $1 million prize to the person who comes up with a practical way to make test-tube meat by 2012. Many PETA activists object to the idea of eating animal tissue even if no animals are killed in its production. On its Web site PETA explains why it is sponsoring the contest:

> More than 40 billion chickens, fish, pigs, and cows are killed every year for food in the United States in horrific ways. Chickens

are drugged to grow so large they often become crippled, mother pigs are confined to metal cages so small they can't move, and fish are hacked apart while still conscious—all to feed America's meat addiction. In vitro meat would spare animals from this suffering. In addition, in vitro meat would dramatically reduce the devastating effects the meat industry has on the environment.

PETA, "PETA Offers $1 Million Reward to First to Make In Vitro Meat." www.peta.org/feat_in_vitro_contest.asp.

many PETA members object to eating anything that even resembles meat, regardless of how it is produced.

By-Product: The Organic Food Movement

One by-product of the availability of genetically modified foods—unintentional on the part of the biotechnology industry—is the growing organic food movement. Before the end of the decade, sales of organic foods are projected to exceed $32 billion. That is still a small fraction of overall food-sales, but the annual growth of the market for organic foods far outpaces the growth of the market for conventional foods.

The market growth for organic foods is much greater than that for conventional foods because of the widespread mistrust of genetic engineering.

One reason the public chooses to buy organic foods is the guarantee that food labeled "organic" contains no genetically engineered ingredients. Since genetically engineered foods do not require labels, consumers have no way of knowing which foods contain genetically modified ingredients. Some communities in northern California have even declared themselves GMO free. The towns of Santa Cruz, Arcata, and Pt. Arena as well as Mendocino, Marin, and Trinity counties have all banned genetically engineered foods from their markets. The ban of GE foods by entire towns illustrates a widespread mistrust of these products. Many people are willing to pay extra to guarantee that the foods they buy are GMO free.

Some Obstacles to Overcome

Though the FDA does not consider public opinion when it makes decisions about the safety of food, public opinion does impact research. Since the goal of biotech companies is to market their products, they must consider whether future profits justify the expense of the research. David Stark, a vice president at Monsanto, estimates that bringing a new product from research and development to market takes an average of ten years and $100 million. Many obstacles must be overcome before genetically modified foods hit the shelves.

FRANKENFOODS: SAFE FOR ANIMALS?

"We know that many consumers are leery of 'Frankenfoods,' but genetically engineered crops and microorganisms are already widely used. Producers will have to show that the inserted genes do not harm the animal's health and that any food from a genetically engineered animal is safe to eat." —*New York Times* editorial.

New York Times, "Coming to a Plate Near You," editorial, October 3, 2008. www.ny times.com/2008/10/04/opinion/04sat3.html.

Aside from rulings by the FDA, biotech companies must overcome public resistance—sometimes called the "yuck factor."

Genetically modified foods are often referred to as "Frankenfoods," a reference to the fictional character Dr. Frankenstein, who constructed a monster in his laboratory. Those who oppose GMOs voice concerns about the environment and fears that once unleashed, GMO foods will overrun the ecosystem, eliminate biodiversity, and create super strains that choke out the competition.

END THE WAR AGAINST NATURE

"There is a fundamental question here: Is progress really just about marching forward? We say no. We say it is time to stop assuming that discoveries only move us forward. The war against nature has to end. And we are going to stop it." —Lord Melchett, former executive director of Greenpeace, UK.

Quoted in Michael Specter, "The Pharmageddon Riddle," *New Yorker*, April 10, 2000, p. 58.

That fear is voiced frequently about corn, for example, known in Mexico as maize. Small fields of ancient varieties of corn, called landraces, are cultivated throughout Mexico just as they have been for ten thousand years. In recent years, scientists have confirmed that genetically engineered corn has crept into these remote cornfields without the farmers' knowledge or intent.

Butterflies, Frogs, Fish, and Caddis Flies

The effects of genetically engineered plants and animals on ecosystems can be far-reaching. Not only are scientists beginning to understand that genes interact with each other in unpredictable ways, they also cannot predict how each ecosystem involved may be affected. For example, a study by a team of environmental scientists at Indiana University found that water runoff from fields of genetically engineered *Bt* corn is washing into streams near other cornfields. The high levels of the toxin intended for the corn borer, a caterpillar, is also reducing the population of caddis flies, insects related to the corn borer. The reduction of caddis flies, in turn, deprives the fish and amphibians that feed on this insect. The birds that feed on the fish and amphibians also suffer. Not all scientists, however, accept this perspective.

In 1999 the public was outraged by a report in the highly respected scientific journal *Nature* that populations of monarch butterflies were threatened by eating milkweed dusted with pollen from nearby *Bt* corn. The newspapers were filled with dire predictions about the destruction of the butterfly. Three years later, new studies found that the danger to the butterfly was actually minimal in real-world conditions outside the laboratory. However, that information was barely noted by news organizations and ignored by the public.

Perhaps most telling, the monarch butterfly story illustrates how difficult it is to find the truth when each side has so much

A report published in 1999 claimed that populations of monarch butterflies were threatened by eating milkweed dusted with pollen from nearby Bt *corn. It was later determined that any threat to the butterflies was minimal.*

to gain from its perspective. The Pew Initiative on Food and Biotechnology, a nonprofit, nonpartisan organization, published a report in 2002 titled *Genetically Engineered Corn and the Monarch Butterfly*. The report examines the background of the monarch butterfly story and how timing, special interests, science, politics, and industry converged to magnify a small story into an international sensation. The public was left with the impression that monarch butterflies are threatened, even though later studies—not as well publicized—did not bear that out. The report also highlights how "eventually, with the leadership of the U.S. Department of Agriculture (USDA), scientists from government, industry, academia, and environmental groups worked together to develop a consensus set of experiments needed to answer the question of whether genetically engineered corn posed a risk."[17] It details the process of how the groups worked together so that each was satisfied that its concerns were addressed.

Can the Price of Resistance Get Too High?

The passionate objection to genetically engineered foods may be showing signs of softening, and science and politics are only partly responsible. As food and energy prices rise, many countries can no longer afford the luxury of boycotting products that contain GMOs. When leaders must decide between philosophical objections and real hunger, their choices are limited.

SOLUTION FOR THE FOOD CRISIS

"The food crisis is much in the news. It is also on the minds of the biotech industry, which is using rising food worries to suggest, contrary to the evidence, that genetically engineered, or GE crops, are needed to help the world feed itself." —Doug Gurian-Sherman, senior scientist at the Union of Concerned Scientists, Washington, D.C.

Doug Gurian-Sherman, "Genetic Engineering—a Crop of Hyperbole," *San Diego Union-Tribune*, June 18, 2008, p. B7.

Much of the world's corn crop lately has been diverted into producing biofuels, resulting in shortages of corn crops grown for food. Prices of rice and wheat have doubled in recent years, also resulting in global hardship. In some countries, farmers cannot afford even to buy the rice they farm.

Strict regulation of GE crops also creates hardships for livestock producers because of the rise in the cost of feed. Feed makers and livestock producers in Europe in 2007 challenged strict rules that forbid the import of grain from the United States if it contains even trace amounts of GE products. They asked that these tight restrictions be relaxed when small amounts of GE corn turned up in tests of corn gluten intended for animal feed.

An article in the *New York Times* claims that Japan and South Korea have resorted to buying GE corn for use in soft drinks, snacks, and other foods, since prices for conventional corn have tripled recently. Steve Mercer, a spokesman for U.S. Wheat Associates, a federally supported cooperative that promotes U.S. wheat abroad, says, "I think it's pretty clear that price and supply concerns have people thinking a little bit differently today."[18] Though outspoken interests are at work on all sides of the GE issue, food shortages and rising prices have begun to chip away at long-standing resistance.

The Tangled Web

As these examples make clear, the most pervasive challenge in genetic engineering, as in many new areas of science, is distinguishing the science from the politics. As the report from the Pew Initiative on Food and Biotechnology explains, it is difficult to sort out the tangled and complicated web of interests that control how, when, and if genetically engineered foods will gain acceptance by the general public.

Basic mistrust of new science and suspicions about the motivations of large biotechnology companies partly fuel the concerns of those who oppose genetically engineered foods. While those concerns may not be voiced outright, they underlie much of the criticism leveled at these products and the companies that promote them. Dyson points out that people might react differently to genetically engineered foods if the field were not driven by huge biotech companies overseen by government agencies.

THE RIGHT TO KNOW WHAT YOU EAT

"To the Editor:
Re: 'Coming to a Plate Near You,' surveys clearly show that the vast majority of Americans want genetically engineered animals to be labeled as such. By not requiring labeling, the FDA will take away a consumer's right to know and right to choose what she eats." —Michael Hansen, senior scientist, Consumer's Union, October 6, 2008.

He compares the current controversy over genetic engineering to mistrust of the early computer industry. In the 1970s computers were mysterious and massive. They occupied entire buildings on university campuses; students would turn in punch cards with data in the morning and return in the afternoon to pick up their results. Dyson notes that in a similar way, large pharmaceutical companies and agribusinesses such as Monsanto

Greenpeace activists in the Philippines denounce Monsanto's Bt corn, saying it requires more fertilizer and therefore causes environmental damage that has cost the country $1 billion per year to repair.

drive and pay for most genetic engineering research. He explains: "The public mistrusts Monsanto because Monsanto likes to put genes for poisonous pesticides into food crops. It is likely that genetic engineering will remain unpopular and controversial so long as it remains a centralized activity in the hands of large corporations."[19]

Dyson continues by reminding readers that the public began to accept computers as they became more familiar and user-friendly. It was not that long ago that consumers eyed frozen foods and cake mixes with suspicion, too. Some food purists believed that advances in food preservation, such as refrigeration and canning, spelled doom for good cooking and fresh foods. In the same way, over time, genetic engineering may become just another tool to improve the foods available at the local grocery store. No one will give it a second thought.

FROM FABRIC
TO FUEL

While it makes sense to have qualms about eating foods with built-in weed and bug killers, controversies about genetically engineered products extend beyond grocery stores and pharmacies. Genetically engineered products now find themselves on fashion runways and inside fuel tanks. As the technology advances, the applications widen. And, just as genetically engineered foods and drugs have both critics and proponents, genetically engineered textiles and energy sources also inspire heated debate.

Sometimes the reasons are familiar: the alleged inability to contain genetically engineered organisms, the dangers they may pose to the environment, and fear of venturing into uncharted frontiers. Sometimes questions are aesthetic: Do people want to wear clothing made from genes that do not match those in nature? Sometimes the questions involve right and wrong: Is it ethical to use foodstuffs to fuel factories and automobiles while people go hungry? These questions occupy the thoughts of scientists, politicians, and the public, who struggle to reconcile interests that may be in conflict. Health, profits, and the search for alternative energy are issues that continue to drive genetic engineering technology.

Itsy Bits of Spider

Genetic engineering is a relatively new science, and it already offers hope of granting some very old human wishes. Humans cannot yet fly like birds, but they are now learning to weave webs like spiders. Though the nearly transparent threads of a spider's web seem fragile, that delicacy is an illusion. Spider silk is actually one of the world's strongest natural materials. Its strength relative to its size is five times that of steel.

The biotech industry hopes to mine that strength for profit by engineering the gene responsible for spider silk into the DNA of goats. When the goats mature, they secrete the protein responsible for spider silk in their milk, creating a product dubbed "milk silk." The protein is then purified, spun into silk, and used to manufacture lightweight materials that require strength and flexibility—just like a spider's web.

According to Michael Fumento, author of *BioEvolution: How Biotechnology Is Changing Our World*, a woven cable of this material as thick as a man's thumb can bear the weight of a 747 airliner. In fact, transferring the gene into a goat, he claims, "allows a single animal to produce more silk protein than the most horrifying mass of big, furry, writhing spiders you can imagine."[20]

The product has many possible uses, some of which have already been tried. Named BioSteel by Nexia Biotechnologies, the company that has combined these unlikely genetic elements, this

By engineering the spider-silk gene into the DNA of goats, which then secrete the protein in their milk, the biotech industry can purify the "milk silk" and spin it into fabrics requiring strength and flexibility.

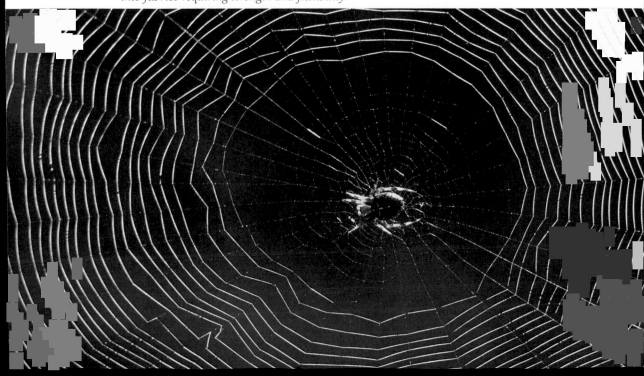

material can be used to make biodegradable fishing lines and nets, surgical sutures, even replacement ligaments and tendons. Its most exciting use, however, may lie not in catching big fish, but in stopping big bullets.

Current lightweight body armor is made with a material called Kevlar that is manufactured by the Dupont Company. But even Kevlar armor is not sufficient to prevent mortal injuries as the weapons become more lethal. BioSteel fabric may be one solution. Soldiers are more likely to wear protective body armor that is comfortable. A vest made of BioSteel spider silk is only a little thicker than nylon, according to Lawrence Osborne, whose report appeared in the *New York Times Magazine* in 2002.

MOSTLY GOATS

"You could call them Spidergoats. But that would give people misconceptions. They're only 1/70,000th spider, after all. When it comes down to it, they're just normal goats with one spider gene in them. They're just goats. Mostly." —Jeffrey D. Turner, chief executive officer, Nexia Technologies.

Quoted in Lawrence Osborne, "Got Silk," *New York Times*, June 16, 2002. http://query.ny times.com/gst/fullpage.html?sec=health&res=9C05E7DD113DF935A25755C0A9649C8 B63&scp=1&sq=Got%20Silk%20Lawrence%20Osborne&st=cse.

Though the goats with their new genes graze calmly on Nexia's farms in rural Quebec, Canada, the spiders themselves do not fare so well. Nexia uses two common spiders—a garden spider and a golden orb weaver native to the tropics. The spiders are flash frozen in liquid nitrogen and then ground into powder. The silk-producing genes are then extracted from the spider powder. These genes are engineered with a genetic switch that is programmed to turn on only when excreted in the milk of a female goat. Finally, the new genes are implanted in the eggs of nanny goats. Since the DNA of a goat consists of 70,000 genes, these "Spidergoats" are only one/seventy-thousandth spider. Once the nanny goats give birth, the spider genes switch on and the goat milk is fortified with spider silk protein.

A Dyeing Art

The ancient Chinese art of silk dyeing is getting an update. For more than five thousand years, artists in China have dyed silk with natural dyes. A pigment excreted by a marine snail, for example, is responsible for the royal purple silk that signified royalty. The Japanese adapted silk to make the traditional kimonos. Silk gained popularity in Europe when Marco Polo carried it back from his journey to the Far East in the 1200s. Silkworm cocoons vary in color from white, yellow, straw, salmon, pink, and green depending on the pigments present in the mulberry leaves, the silkworm's natural diet. Now, Takashi Sakudoh, from the University of Tokyo, reported that he was able to genetically engineer silkworms to control the color of their cocoons. He and his research team observed that silkworms that produce white cocoons have a genetic mutation. By engineering that mutation into normal silkworms, they were able to vary the colors of the cocoon, producing red, flesh-color, and vivid yellow cocoons. Silk dyeing could become a dying art. Sakudoh's paper was published in the *Proceedings of the National Academy of Sciences of the United States* in May 2007.

By engineering a mutation into normal silkworms, scientists were able to vary the colors of a silkworm's cocoon, producing red, flesh-color, and vivid yellow cocoons.

The tricky part of the process, however, is figuring out exactly how spiders spin the silk. Spiders produce up to seven kinds of silk proteins. Each protein is spun inside the spider's abdomen in a different way. Spiders use one silk to build the web's diagonal support lines and another to construct its inner wheels. So far, the BioSteel product is made with only one protein.

Nexia's president and chief executive officer, Jeffrey D. Turner, is excited about the future prospects for his company. He says, "It's nothing short of a revolution. This special silk is the first transgenic material ever made. The amazing thing, however, is that we're changing the world from a tiny low-rent sugar farm, and our only machinery is a goat."[21] One advantage to producing silk rather than pharmaceuticals, he explains, is that FDA approval is not required before the material goes to market.

Mary's Little Lamb's Thick Fleece

If spider silk can be genetically engineered into goat's milk, then genetically engineering sheep with thicker fleece might seem straightforward. In Australia, where sheep farming is common, the results of a three-year study completed by Commonwealth Scientific and Industrial Research Organization (CSIRO) Livestock Industries showed, however, that big, wooly sheep also had big problems. Researchers there engineered various breeds of sheep with an extra growth hormone gene and monitored the results.

Though some of the sheep did grow larger and produce thicker fleece, their hooves grew too fast, and they were prone to diabetes. Moreover, not every breed of sheep reacted in the same way to the extra gene. Merino sheep produced more wool, while the Poll Dorset breed produced less. In some sheep the extra gene was present but not expressed in a noticeable way.

Researchers also found that the GM sheep had more problems with parasites. This challenge may be overcome by genetically engineering sheep that produce an insecticide on their own skin. Scientists are also working to create sheep with wool that does not shrink and is more elastic and stronger than conventional wool. Since only one hundred sheep were involved in the CSIRO study, the results are still preliminary.

Genetic Engineering Backlash: Organic Fiber

Cotton, however, is the crop with the greatest impact on the fashion industry. By the end of the first decade of the twenty-first century, half of the world's cotton crop will consist of *Bt* cotton, genetically engineered, like corn and soybeans, to resist pests. Though this might appear harmless enough to people, critics fear that controlling resistant strains of pests will require ever-stronger poisons. Aside from the danger to food crops growing nearby, these poisons might endanger the health of workers in the field. Much of the cotton used worldwide is grown in countries where workers are not protected by strict laws governing exposure to toxic chemicals. Ten million people in west central Africa alone depend on growing and processing cotton.

Public distrust of genetically engineered cotton also fuels the growing popularity of organically grown textiles. One designer, Katherine Hamnett, has taken the lead in the movement to grow and use organic cotton. She was inspired by a trip to Africa in

This farm in Clarksdale, Mississippi, consists mostly of Bt *cotton, which resists pests. Critics fear that resistant strains of pests will require even stronger poisons to control them.*

2003, when she observed firsthand how cotton growers struggle to survive.

It is difficult for African cotton farmers to compete in the world market when farmers in the United States are paid subsidies by the government to produce more cotton than they can sell. The resulting surplus drives down the cost of imported cotton. While visiting Africa, Hamnett befriended the wife of a cotton farmer in Mali who had lost three of her seven children to malnutrition, since her husband could barely support his family by growing cotton.

Hamnett decided to take action. She convinced the Mali government to allow Oxfam, a worldwide nongovernmental agency that works to combat global hunger and poverty, to run a model farm to grow organic cotton. Hamnett's aims are lofty. She hopes that growing organic cotton with traditional farming techniques will accomplish two important goals: help preserve the social and cultural structure of life in Mali and provide enough cotton to sustain the economy there.

One danger to poor farmers posed by genetically modified cotton is the control wielded by the holder of the GE patent. Farmers are forced to buy new seed each year rather than plant seed from the previous year's crop. Subsidized cotton crops in the United States and patents held by large corporations threaten the livelihoods of farmers and the future of farming itself in these small, economically fragile communities.

Moreover, Hamnett, a world-renowned clothing designer, has a loud voice in the fashion world. She explains how her passion fuels her goals: "Look, I've done the Paris shows, where all these people come backstage and air-kiss and say they loved the line, and I'm just trying to control my face because I don't give a damn. That life never gave me the kind of high I got when Pesticide Action Network (PAN UK) and the Soil Association agreed to train organic cotton farmers in Mali."[22] Hamnett was once named British Designer of the Year, though her political actions have angered many high-ranking British officials.

Patagonia Takes a Side

Other clothing companies are also lining up to oppose genetic engineering, even if they do not have a direct connection to genetically engineered products. In 2002 Patagonia, a major outdoor clothing supplier, publicly renounced *Bt* corn and Roundup Ready soybeans. Yvon Chouinard, the founder and owner of Patagonia, issued a statement in 2002 in which he said, "For humans to adopt every new technology just because we can is irresponsible, especially when a new technology puts us up against an edge that's hard to see, feel, or even define. New technologies, like genetically engineered food, should be considered unsafe until proven otherwise, not the other way around."[23]

In the same essay, Chouinard explains the "Precautionary Principle," which states that if an activity might threaten safety, precautionary measures should be taken even if not all cause-and-effect relationships are fully understood. In other words, the burden of proof lies with the individual or the company that is taking the action, not with the public that might suffer unknown consequences.

The Precautionary Principle drives Chouinard's support for organic fibers, such as cotton, since genetic engineering and chemicals—with effects that are not fully understood—are routinely used in cotton production. Furthermore, cotton is only one fiber that benefits from the public distaste for genetic engineering. Linen, produced from flax, hemp—a fast-growing plant similar to flax—and jute are also gaining popularity as organic fabrics move from hippie to hip.

Biodegradable Plastic for Any Occasion

The growing popularity and availability of a textile that begins as corn, some of which may be genetically engineered, presents a dilemma for many consumers who pride themselves on their reliance on eco-friendly products but tend to avoid products they consider unnatural. A material whose very name implies unnatural, a plastic called polyactide (PLA), is manufactured in the United States by NatureWorks LLC in a multistep process that begins with simple cornstarch.

NatureWorks concedes that some of that corn is genetically engineered but assures consumers that no genetic material remains in the finished product. The cornstarch is used to make dextrose, a sugar, which is then fermented and turned into lactic

Polyactide, a material that looks and feels like plastic, is made from corn through the refinement of cornstarch.

acid in a process similar to that used to make beer or wine. Further refinement results in a material that has been named Ingeo. Though it looks and feels like plastic, it is actually fully biodegradable, since it is made from corn. NatureWorks LLC then licenses other companies to provide finished products to consumers.

Corn and Soybean Digest published an article in 2006 titled "Wear Your Corn Crop," which described Ingeo's growing popularity. Everything from sheets, pillowcases, and blankets to socks, hosiery, men's suits, and women's dresses are constructed with this human-made material constructed from a natural product. And, like plastic, Ingeo can be rigid or pliable, clear or opaque, depending on the manufacturing process used. Unlike plastic, however, Ingeo can be tilled back into the soil at the end of its useful life to fertilize the next generation of corn. Ingeo debuted in the fashion world in 2003, and four years later over six hundred retail outlets, including Target and Wal-Mart, featured products made with the biodegradable material. Ingeo can also be fashioned into packaging materials, carpet, upholstery filling, and hard "plastic" items such as golf tees and cutlery.

Body-Odor Eaters

As if manufacturing clothing from cornstarch is not outlandish enough, scientists are also working to genetically engineer bacteria that feast on human sweat and dirt. As they learn how to infuse certain fibers such as cotton with bacteria, scientists may soon develop the technology to produce clothing that cleans it-self. Genetically engineered *E. coli*, the bacteria associated with upset stomachs, may soon be feasting on the proteins that cause the stink in smelly clothing.

An article written by five scientists at the University of Massachusetts at Dartmouth explains why clothing is the ideal habitat for cells genetically designed to perform functions associated with the human body: "Clothing materials are generally bio-friendly (nontoxic to cells); sources of heat, moisture and even nutrients are all readily available from the human body."[24] The same technology may also one day enable the development of bandages that produce their own healing medications and fabrics that are water repellent or glow in the dark. These functions and others will be performed by bacteria that have been genetically tweaked and powered solely by human body waste and then built right into the structure of the fabric itself. These features are now sometimes added after the item is manufactured.

Using Genetics to Fill the Gas Tank

Though genetically engineered clothing is currently a gimmick for the elite consumer, designer fuels are finding a market with energy producers desperate to find alternatives to fuels made from petroleum. Biotechnology companies are genetically engineering corn and other crops to produce ethanol and other biofuels, a solution that entails growing rather than drilling. Ethanol is a form of alcohol similar to that found in alcoholic beverages. In the United States ethanol is usually made from corn, though other countries, such as Brazil, use sugarcane. Soybeans and prairie grass are also used.

The process of converting corn into ethanol involves the addition of amylase, an enzyme, at the ethanol factory. Amylase breaks cornstarch down into sugar, which is then fermented and processed into ethanol. Syngenta, a biotechnology company based in North Carolina, has genetically engineered a corn plant that eliminates the need to add amylase.

Syngenta worked with another biotechnology company— Diversa in California—to combine three amylase genes from bacteria that thrive near hot-water vents on the ocean floor. By inserting these genes into corn plants, each corn kernel becomes, in effect, a self-contained amylase factory. Since the enzyme is derived from bacteria that thrive on heat, ethanol factories can operate at higher temperatures, increasing efficiency.

Biofuel Critics

Right now, however, the process is not efficient enough to offset dependence on foreign oil. An article in the *New York Times* explains the issue that faces ethanol proponents: "Even if the nation's entire corn crop were converted to ethanol production, it would replace only about 15 percent of the nation's transportation fuel needs, according to an Energy Department report."[25] However, though everyone agrees that the search for new fuel sources is urgent, the rapid growth of biofuel crops has powerful critics.

One question that is raised with increasing alarm is whether growing food crops to produce energy is creating a global food crisis as demand for corn increases and prices rise. The Earth Policy Institute, an environmental group, reported in 2007 that nearly eighty ethanol plants are under construction and could soon consume as much as half of the corn crop—genetically engineered or otherwise—cultivated in the United States alone. Calling it a "furious gold rush," an article in the *New York Times* placed responsibility for the sudden increase on a call by the

Biotechnology companies are genetically engineering corn and other crops to produce ethanol and other biofuels, a solution that entails growing rather than drilling. Many vehicles can now run on "flex fuel," or E-85, as it is known at the pump.

Rising Food Prices and Biofuels

While biofuels offer some hope of reducing dependence on foreign oil, they have other consequences that do not bode well for the global community. The World Bank, an international organization, issued a report in July 2008 blaming biofuel production for rising food prices. In fact, it reported that 100 million people have been pushed below the poverty line as a result. The U.S. government, on the other hand, links climbing food prices to higher standards of living in developing countries, which increases demand for food. Over one-third of corn grown in the United States alone is now used to produce ethanol, a fuel additive. In addition, about half of the vegetable oils in the European Union are used to produce biodiesel, another fuel. Farmers worldwide are encouraged to set aside land for biofuel production. Also, the growing market for grain encourages speculation, which also drives up prices. Supporters point to the environmental benefits of biofuels, but some experts are not convinced. David King, the government's former chief scientific adviser, responded to the World Bank report by saying: "It is clear that some biofuels have huge impacts on food prices. All we are doing by supporting these is subsidizing higher food prices, while doing nothing to tackle climate change."

Quoted in Aditya Chakrabortty, "Secret Report: Biofuels Caused Food Crisis," Global Policy Forum, July 4, 2008. www.globalpolicy.org/socecon/hunger/general/2008/0407secret.htm.

George W. Bush administration to produce renewable fuels and curb America's reliance on foreign oil.

Politicians from rural farming states join the push to grow corn for fuel, since the effort raises local incomes and benefits their states' economies. The National Corn Growers Association and the Renewable Fuels Association express belief that record harvests ensure enough corn for every purpose. However, Lester Brown, president of the Earth Policy Institute, counters that diverting corn to fuel production cannot help but affect food prices, as the cost of feeding livestock leads to higher prices for meat, poultry, and dairy products. He has called for a federal moratorium on licensing new ethanol factories, while experts weigh the pros and cons of diverting corn crops to ethanol. Like any new technology, it is impossible to plan for every possibility.

Each scientific advance has unforeseen consequences, some of which are positive and others negative.

Another fear is the same that critics voice about any technology that involves genetically engineered food crops—the possibility that the corn modified for ethanol production will accidentally contaminate food crops. Regardless of whether that airborne pollen rises from crops grown for drugs or fuel, the distaste for eating ingredients not intended for human consumption is widespread. Proponents argue, however, that risk of contamination is minimal and far outweighed by the benefits of growing rather than drilling for fuel. Furthermore, they point out, fields of growing grains actually absorb carbon dioxide, a gas released into the atmosphere by automobiles and factories and widely blamed for global warming.

One biotechnology company is working on a solution to the problem of cross-contamination. Sustainable Oil is a joint venture by two companies: Green Earth Fuels, which manufactures biodiesel fuel, and Targeted Growth, which develops genetically engineered plants. Targeted Growth has genetically engineered the camelina plant to produce seeds with 20 percent more oil than seeds from conventional plants. That oil is then processed into biodiesel fuel. Furthermore, although the camelina plant is a distant relative of canola, a plant used to make cooking oil and other products, humans do not eat camelina itself, which means that they will not unintentionally ingest it.

Camelina cultivation has other benefits. Since it thrives on parched, dry land, the crop benefits farmers who live in regions that depend on artificial irrigation to water their crops. Within the next few years, farmers in Montana, for example, expect to grow enough "Elite Camelina" to produce 100 million gallons of biodiesel each year.

Biodiesel fuel has become popular in recent years as consumers have become increasingly aware of the dangers inherent in carbon dioxide emissions. Biodiesel fuel produces almost 80 percent less carbon dioxide than regular diesel. Moreover, most vehicles that use regular diesel fuel can use biodiesel with minimal modifications. Ethanol, on the other hand, is far less efficient. Ethanol must be mixed into gasoline in various concentrations, and most cars cannot run on ethanol alone.

Still, Targeted Growth must answer to critics who object to genetic engineering altogether. Responding to those critics, Tom Todaro, the CEO of the company, told CNET News.com recently, "One of my favorite stats is that more people are killed by falling Coke machines every year than [by] genetically modified foods. Eighty percent of the corn and soy sold worldwide has biotech inside of it. You ate a transgene at breakfast this morning if you had cereal; I guarantee it."[26]

Another nonfood-to-fuel solution may be the cultivation of certain grasses, such as switch grass, which, like camelina, is low maintenance. Genetic engineers are developing strains of plants with less lignin, the substance that makes plants stiff but also interferes with the process of converting the plant into ethanol. This prospect, however, alarms environmentalists who foresee

Turning Algae into Fuel

In July 2008 Chris Ladd, a writer for *Popular Mechanics* magazine, interviewed geneticist J. Craig Venter. Known as a maverick, Venter is both envied and admired for his independence and ability to forge ahead and realize his goals. He was the first to map the human genome and is now working on a project to produce biofuels by genetically engineering algae. He is hopeful that genetic engineering will provide a way to replace the current necessity of mining 30 billion barrels of oil and 3 billion tons of coal from the earth each year.

Ladd: "Where do you see the science of genetics going in the near future?"

Venter: "I see it as parallel to the electronics industry in the 1940s and '50s, a stage when all of the things that enabled computers came out of just a few handfuls of components—resistors, transistors, capacitors—and people were pretty much limited only by their imagination. My team has discovered more than 20 million new genes, so we're in a biological universe. There are no fundamental limits. I think we're going to see the next 25 years as some of the most innovative in the history of science."

Quoted in Chris Ladd, "10 Big Questions for Maverick Geneticist J. Craig Venter on America's Energy Future," *Popular Mechanics*, July 30, 2008. www.popularmechanics.com/blogs/science_news/4275738.html.

forests filled with drooping trees that have cross-pollinated with lignin-deficient plants.

A Genetic Visionary

"Utilizing biology we have the ability to address every area of our lives—from medical treatment, to renewable sources of fuels. Plastics, carpets, clothing, medicines and motor oil—all of these things can be created by biological organisms, and in a safe, environmentally sustainable manner." —J. Craig Venter, geneticist.

J. Craig Venter, "Taking Control of Biology," *San Diego Union-Tribune*, June 20, 2008. www.signonsandiego.com/uniontrib/20080620/news_lz1e20venter.html.

The applications of genetic engineering have just begun to show up in food, drugs, fashion, and fuel. Someday humankind may look back at the beginning of the twenty-first century and wonder why people worried about some of the things that now concern them and missed some of the problems that no one imagined. Dyson outlines the five questions that he believes must be addressed as biotechnology moves from the outward fringes of science into the everyday lives of ordinary people: "First, can it be stopped? Second, ought it to be stopped? Third, if stopping it is either impossible or undesirable, what are the appropriate limits that our society must impose on it? Fourth, how should the limits be decided? Fifth, how should the limits be enforced, nationally and internationally?"[27] Dyson does not answer these questions. Instead, he says, he leaves the solutions to his children and grandchildren. Students who are now in elementary school and their parents are those children and grandchildren to whom Dyson refers. Dyson believes that everyone shares in the responsibility to understand genetic engineering and to voice opinions about how this powerful technology is applied.

DESIGNER BABIES

While controversy swirls around genetically engineered fuels and fashion, those controversies pale next to arguments that rage about the genetic engineering of humans. These modifications might involve deleting genes known to result in inheritable diseases. Or they might involve adding genes identified with certain traits. Those traits could be cosmetic, such as eye and hair color, or involve abilities and talents, such as musicianship, intelligence, or athleticism. In either case, clouds of controversy accumulate each time another sequence of bases—adenine, thymine, guanine, and cytosine—is linked to a specific trait. Each time a sequence is identified, the question central to the genetic engineering of humans is raised: How much control should humans assume over the information that creates babies with or without certain traits? Dyson's questions about the future of genetic engineering become most urgent when considering the lives of human beings, particularly since these decisions affect the lives of children, the most vulnerable and least powerful human beings.

Designer Babies: The New Fashion Trend

In 2008 the first baby conceived in a test tube celebrated her thirtieth birthday. At the time, the birth of Louise Brown was headline news around the world. Childless couples desperate to have a family had newfound hope. However, the rapidly growing science of genetics may soon provide parents with options that no one even imagined thirty years ago.

One day, people may be able to choose how tall their child will become, or what color eyes and hair that child will have, or even how intelligent and talented he or she may be. An article in

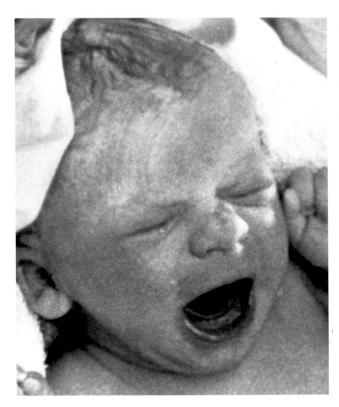

Louise Joy Brown, the world's first test-tube baby, was born in 1978. At the time, people were questioning the ethics of this medical breakthrough.

Time magazine compared the future possibilities to a shopping trip: "Before the new millennium is many years old, parents may be going to fertility clinics and picking from a list of options the way car buyers order air conditioning and chrome-alloy wheels."[28] This tendency to compare the selection of a baby's genetic traits to a shopping trip, and even the term "designer babies" itself, hints at genetic engineering's greatest obstacle. Many people simply do not believe it is right to pick and choose the details of a child as if he or she were a fashion accessory.

While the topic of designer babies often arises when genetic engineering is discussed, the reality is that adding to or changing the genes in an embryo's sperm or egg cells—known as germ cells—are advances yet to be realized. Germ-line manipulation is the scientific term given to changing an embryo's DNA so that an embryo will inherit traits that might then be passed along to future children. This is the genetic engineering people most associate with designer babies.

Critics, however, voice serious concerns. Society places great importance on unconditional parental love. In 2004 Michael Sandel, a Harvard philosopher, published an essay titled "The Case Against Perfection: Ethics in the Age of Genetic Engineering." In that essay Sandel weighs parents' rights to make genetic choices against the dangers of making such choices. Sandel warns that society suffers when children are viewed like products, with some children—and some traits—considered more valuable than others.

Other writers also refer to Sandel's essay to help clarify their ideas about genetic engineering. Mike Polyakov, a graduate student at the University of California at Berkeley, for example, disagrees with Sandel's belief that parents should have choice about some aspects of their children's genetic makeup, such as predisposition to certain diseases, but not others. "One can't condemn parents for choosing a smarter or taller than average child on these grounds, for they can reasonably say they are doing it entirely for the child's good."[29]

LIMITLESS POSSIBILITIES

"Anything that I can imagine in terms of changing genes in a baby, I could do. I could give a baby the hearing ability of a dog or the eyesight of a hawk." —Lee Silver, geneticist.

Quoted in *Frontpage*, "Back to the Future," BBC News, December 1999. http://news .bbc.co.uk/hi/english/static/ special_report/1999/12/99/back_to_the_future/lee_silver.stm.

For the sake of argument, he assumes that everyone has equal access to these genetic benefits. He also points out that what people consider "normal" varies. A condition considered normal in the jungles of the tropics, for example, may be dysfunctional in the Arctic. Abstract concepts such as beauty and intelligence also vary widely from one culture to another.

Breeding Better Babies: Good Idea or Not?

Another issue that simmers close to the surface in discussions about genetic engineering is eugenics, a social movement that was promoted mostly in the nineteenth and twentieth centuries.

Sir Francis Galton (1822–1911) was a British scientist who coined the term eugenics. *He believed in improving the human race by allowing only those with desirable genetic traits to bear children.*

Eugenics, which comes from the Greek prefix *eu*, meaning "good," and the root *gen*, meaning "birth," involves improvement of the human race by allowing only those with desired genetic traits to bear children.

Before genes were deliberately engineered, eugenics advocates promoted the sterilization of people who had traits considered undesirable. Moreover, they favored the deliberate selection of mothers and fathers to breed superior children. Nowadays, most people associate eugenics with Nazi policies during World War II. At that time, the Nazis killed many people who did not have traits they considered ideal, such as blond hair and blue eyes. Eugenics is considered an extreme example of how genetic engineering might be abused.

PARENTS MAKE CHOICES

"While enhancing a child's height or intellectual potential may not improve his or her life, it is unlikely to be any more damaging than myriads of other choices parents currently make for their children, from the music lessons they force on them, to their diet, to their schools." —Mike Polyakov, political theory graduate student at the University of California–Berkeley.

Mike Polyakov, "The Ethics of Designer Children," Institute for Ethics and Emerging Technologies, April 10, 2008. http://ieet.org/index.php/IEET/more/polyakov20080410.

Polyakov offers a compromise. He suggests that individual parents should be free to make choices for their own children, while denying those same choices to society as a whole. He reminds readers that genes simply play one role in determining how a child will develop. They do not absolutely determine talents, intelligence, and athletic ability. Parents, siblings, friends, education, and the place where someone is raised are among the many factors—collectively known as "nurture"—that contribute to a child's development. Polyakov ends his essay on a personal note: "And if I was in that position, I would push for the best . . . genes money can buy."[30]

Fixing What Is Genetically Broken

Right now, though, the possibility of genetically engineering super babies remains a figment of popular imagination. Most of the current work in genetic engineering involves manipulating the genes to fix disorders that result when existing genes malfunction. Parkinson's disease, Alzheimer's disease, certain cancers such as leukemia, and diabetes are among the diseases that result when systems regulated by the genes stop functioning correctly.

Several techniques are used for repairing malfunctioning genes. One technique, known as somatic cell manipulation, or more commonly, gene therapy, involves introducing genes into the body to

Here, a scientist prepares culture dishes with gene-corrected cells that may be used for cancer patients or those with inherited blindness.

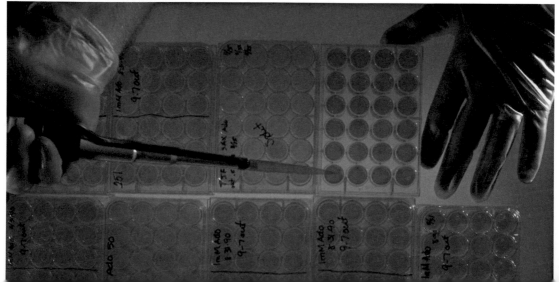

correct faulty messages that certain genes communicate to cells. Genes are actually coded instructions for building proteins, which then perform all the functions within the body. Sometimes, for reasons that are not clearly understood, those instructions go haywire. Tumor growth, for example, is the result of a failure of cells to stop growing.

Gene therapy can take different forms. Sometimes abnormal genes are swapped for healthy ones in the hope the healthy genes will take over and restore normal function. Other times, doctors might actually repair the abnormal gene. It is even possible to adjust chemically the degree to which a gene is turned on or off. An overactive gene can be stabilized, or a sluggish gene can be chemically induced to function more efficiently.

Gene therapy that involves replacement genes presents additional challenges, however. These replacement genes, which act as tiny repair kits, are carried into the cells by a molecule—usually a virus—that also has been genetically altered to accomplish its task. Some fear that the altered viruses may recover their original ability to cause disease and wreak havoc on immune systems that are already weakened. People sometimes develop immune responses to the viruses that carry the new genes. Furthermore, since cells constantly replace themselves, replacement genes must be replenished frequently, which makes gene therapy short-lived and therefore somewhat impractical.

In addition, many conditions such as high blood pressure, Alzheimer's and Parkinson's diseases, diabetes, and arthritis result from the combined effects of several genetic malfunctions. Although this research shows promise, so far the FDA has not approved a single human gene therapy for commercial use.

But in spite of the challenges, gene therapy is progressing. In 2003 researchers at the National Cancer Institute reengineered immune cells to attack cancer cells in patients with an advanced and deadly form of skin cancer. In 2008 British researchers reported in the *New England Journal of Medicine* that eyesight of test subjects with a form of inherited blindness improved after experimental gene therapy. Scientists have recently begun to identify certain gene variations that seem to explain why some people are prone to anxiety, addicted to nicotine, susceptible to AIDS, and more likely to be stricken with aggressive cancers.

Each time scientists identify a genetic variation linked to a disease or disorder, they move closer to learning how to engineer the genes to fix the problems. Successes do not, however, necessarily result in widespread approval. The public and scientists grapple with questions such as: What is normal? What is a disorder? Who decides? Is it ethical to devote so many resources to finding cures for diseases that afflict some people when millions of others suffer from problems such as malnutrition that the same resources might prevent?

Running Faster, Throwing Farther

Ted Friedmann, director of the Center for Molecular Genetics at the University of California at San Diego, pioneers the study of gene therapy to treat serious diseases such as cystic fibrosis, cancer, and immune system deficiencies. Friedmann also leads investigations into gene doping, the term given to gene therapy intended to enhance athletic performance. Unlike performance-enhancing drugs, gene doping involves transferring genes rather than drugs into an athlete's cells or tissues. Because the new genes match the athlete's own, they are undetectable by standard tests. In fact, according to Friedmann, the only way right now to detect gene doping is to study the secondary effects on an athlete's body. The World Anti-Doping Agency works hard

A variation on gene therapy, called gene doping, can be used to enhance an athlete's performance. Instead of the use of performance-enhancing drugs, genes are transferred into an athlete's cells or tissues.

to stay abreast of each new technique devised to cheat the system in competitive sports. Gene doping presents a difficult challenge, but Friedmann is certain that gene doping detection is on the horizon.

Athletics, in fact, is an arena in which the controversy about genetic engineering is often played out. In an essay titled "The Modified Man," distributed by the Center for Genetics and Society, Carl T. Hall, a science writer for the *San Francisco Chronicle*, writes, "Very quickly, scenarios spring up of enhanced trans-humanist superathletes whacking 1,000-foot home runs or throwing 100-yard passes with pinpoint accuracy."[31] Most people are wary of enhancing humans beyond what is considered normal.

Sometimes, however, athletes benefit inadvertently from gene therapy developed for reasons having nothing to do with athletics. Hubert Kim, director of a cartilage repair and regeneration project in San Francisco, for example, is studying how genes regulate muscle degeneration after an injury or surgery. He and his team genetically engineered mice to lack the genes that cause muscles to shrink from disuse after an injury. Though Kim's goal is to help patients recover from surgery more quickly, others envision faster returns to the playing field for highly paid athletes sidelined by injuries.

THE MEANING OF SPORTS

"What matters here is what athletes and the people who watch athletes believe sports to be about. Sports isn't about genetic modifications. If people lose heart and give in to doping, sports will be changed and not for the better." —Thomas H. Murray, president of the Hastings Center, an independent bioethics center.

Quoted in Scott LaFee, "The Race Against Gene Doping," *San Diego Union-Tribune*, July 27, 2008, p. A12.

This is when the lines become blurred between treatment and performance enhancement. Tom Vail, chief of orthopedics at the University of California at San Francisco (UCSF) Medical Center,

Genetic Superstar

Michael Phelps, the U.S. Olympic swimmer who won eight gold medals in 2008, may have a natural genetic edge. According to George Dvorsky, who serves on the board of directors for the Institute for Ethics and Emerging Technologies, Phelps has several inborn features that give him a natural competitive advantage, among them:

- His six-foot seven-inch armspan exceeds his height by a full three inches.

- His size fourteen feet give him a 10 percent advantage over his competition.

- His hands are larger than average, which allows him to move more water.

- His muscles produce 50 percent less lactic acid than other ath-letes, which allows him to work harder for longer periods.

- He is double-jointed in the chest area; this enables him to extend his arms higher above his head and pull down at an angle that increases his efficiency.

These physical advantages fuel the argument by some that gene doping is one way to level the playing field. As Dvorsky points out, "Looking at this list, it's as if Phelps was designed to swim. How could the genetic lottery ever be construed as something that's not arbitrary and unfair?"

George Dvorsky, "Michael Phelps: 'Naturally' Transhuman," Institute for Ethics and Emerging Technologies, August 19, 2008. http://ieet.org/index.php/IEET/more/dvorsky20080818.

American swimmer Michael Phelps has several inborn features that give him a natural competitive advantage. His body seems to have been designed to swim.

is not convinced that a clear distinction can be made between gene therapy and elite, custom, individually tailored training programs. They both boost athletic performance by altering the physiology of individual athletes. Scott LaFee, a reporter for the *San Diego Union-Tribune*, outlines the controversy: "Some observers have argued that gene transfer is OK, that it simply levels the playing field, potentially providing every athlete with roughly the same biological equipment."[32] Not everyone agrees, of course. Thomas H. Murray, president of the Hastings Center, an independent bioethics research center based in New York, believes that gene doping distorts the meaning of sports, which most people believe is about fair play and hard work. However, gene doping promises to be a challenge beyond that posed by testing—or knowing how to cheat the tests—for performance-enhancing drugs.

Happily Ever After Forever

While engineering genetic improvements of babies and adults fascinates the public and scientists alike, the possibility of immortality, or living forever, is a subject that has captured the human imagination since ancient times. The gods and goddesses of ancient Greece and Rome, for example, appeared human but possessed superhuman powers, including immortality. Cynthia Kenyon, a researcher at UCSF, is studying how genetic engineering may actually turn that dream into reality.

In 1993 Kenyon and her team found that changing a specific gene in roundworms doubled the life span of these parasites, which normally live only about three weeks. Their brief life span makes roundworms ideal subjects for aging studies, since tinkering with their genes shows quick results.

The discovery that genetic changes affect life span is monumental because most scientists had assumed that aging is inevitable—the result of cells no longer renewing themselves. In other words, scientists have always assumed that the body simply wears out as time passes. Further studies on other lab animals, including mice, confirmed Kenyon's findings. Furthermore, the same gene that slows aging also seems to protect against cancer and tumor growth. Some scholars predict that human life expectancy could increase to five thousand years in rich countries within the next one hundred years, though others scoff at this notion.

If this technology was applied to athletics, aging sports stars may never retire. However, the ability to control aging may have unintended and potentially devastating consequences to the global economy, health care systems, governments, and the environment. The planet would be hard pressed to support a population that increases unchecked. Nicholas D. Kristof addresses the issue in a *New York Times* editorial: "We are now blundering toward genetic manipulations, a technology that we should embrace—but prudently. It will reshape humanity far more than fire, electricity, space exploration or any other branch of science we have encountered."[33]

Engineering Genetic Monsters

Just as the gods and goddesses of ancient mythology were blessed with immortality, ancient myths foretell other genetic engineering feats. Monsters that are only part human, known collectively as Chimeras, often roam through ancient stories causing trouble. A minotaur, half human and half bull, dines on human flesh

inside a maze. The centaur has the head, arms, and trunk of a human and the body and legs of a horse. An Egyptian sphinx holds its human head high atop the body of a lion. Werewolves terrify with human intelligence that lurks within the bodies of wolves. Mermaids and mermen swim the seas with the heads of humans and the tails of fish. Even the popular fantasy series *Percy Jackson and the Olympians* depends on a character that is half human and half Greek god to create suspense and solve crimes. Chimeras, however, are not just figments of the imagination. Scientists also

A mythical mermaid is considered a Chimera, having the upper body of a human and the lower half of a fish's tail. Scientists create real chimeras through genetic engineering.

create chimeras. These chimeras are real—organisms created by combining the genes of humans and other members of the animal kingdom in the search for answers to problems that plague humankind.

Scientists around the world conduct research on chimeras in order to study human diseases without experimenting on humans. At Stanford University in California, pathologist Irving Weissman has transplanted human brain cells into the brains of mice, for example, in order to study brain cancer. In 2005 Weissman's chimeric mouse brains were 99 percent mouse and 1 percent human. However, he has proposed creating mice with brains that are composed entirely of human brain cells.

GOING TOO FAR

"There are other ways to advance medicine and human health besides going out into the strange, brave new world of chimeric animals. Scientists have now gone over the edge into the pathological domain." —Jeremy Rifkin, biotechnology activist.

Quoted in Maryann Mott, "Animal-Human Hybrids Spark Controversy," *National Geographic News*, January 25, 2005. http://news.nationalgeographic.com/news/2005/01/0125_050125_chimeras.html.

Professor of psychiatry and neurosurgery Eugene Redmond at Yale University is searching for a cure for Parkinson's disease. He and his team inject human nerve cells into the brains of monkeys, hoping the healthy cells will replace the malfunctioning cells that result in the disease's devastating symptoms. Efforts to develop a ready source of organs and blood for human use have resulted in pigs with human blood in their veins, mice with human kidneys, and monkeys with human larynxes. Several years ago, Stuart Newman, professor of cell biology and anatomy at New York Medical College, applied for a patent for a human-ape chimera. His intention was not to create the creature but to alert both the public and the scientific community that gene research was moving in a direction that needed scrutiny.

Could This Happen?

Lee Silver, the Princeton professor known for his outspoken views on genetics, delivered a lecture to a class in 1994 about the genetic similarity of chimpanzees and humans. Soon after, a student approached him to request that Silver become her senior thesis adviser. Her thesis proposal: impregnate herself with the sperm of a chimpanzee and follow the development of the fetus. She planned to terminate the pregnancy before the chimp-human was born. Silver was shocked, but the proposal became the germ of a play he cowrote with Jeremy Karaken, a New York actor and playwright. According to Silver, the play *Sweet, Sweet Motherhood* examines questions such as, "What does it mean to be human and raises a number of ethical and philosophical questions, but it doesn't provide any easy answers." The play leaves unclear whether the student actually becomes pregnant with chimp sperm. The real student, however, never went through with her plan.

Quoted in K.F.G., "Joining Science and Art," *Princeton Alumni Weekly*, October 10, 2007. www.princeton.edu/paw/archive_new/PAW07-08/02-1010/books.html#Books2.

In fact, Newman's patent application was turned down several times for exactly the reasons that concerned him. The U.S. Patent and Trademark Office claimed that some versions of the human-ape chimera were too human to be patented, since the Constitution expressly forbids ownership of human beings. Newman explains that determining how human a chimera has to be before it is considered too human to patent is part of the issue. He says, "Then the question becomes, if we make it so it's only 10 percent human, is that maybe not human enough to be excluded from being patented?"[34] The purpose of combining human cells with those of animals, however, is most often to cultivate a ready source of organs for human transplant.

If It Looks Like a Pig, Does That Make It a Pig?

That goal may soon be realized. Genetic engineering experiments by two researchers, Alan Flake at Children's Hospital in Philadelphia and Esmail Zanjani at the University of Nevada, resulted in the birth of lambs that looked like typical lambs but possessed blood, cartilage, muscles, and hearts that were up to 40 percent human. Israeli scientists have developed a mouse with a tiny functioning human kidney. Lee Silver, a Princeton geneticist, believes that people will accept these creatures as long as they do not appear human in any way. He points out that while people might accept a pig with a human kidney, they would most likely react in horror to a pig with a human arm.

External features are only one part of the debate, however. Many people fear that scientists will create an organism that does not have human features but can think and feel like a human being. If an animal such as a mouse carried inside its head a brain that was completely human, such as that proposed by the Stanford scientist, would this mouse then deserve rights that are solely granted to humans? If the decision that an alert organism with the intelligence and feelings of a human being is not human because it has four legs, a skinny tail, and prefers cheese, then how does society decide who—or what—is human? Silver believes that the boundaries are fuzzy. He compares the human-animal boundary to the color spectrum, in which one color undergoes very gradual changes until, finally, it is identified as another color.

These decisions become increasingly complex if the organism has human features. As scientists master the ability to create human-ape chimeras, the questions and the doubts multiply. Though the scientific community shares the public fear of creating chimeras capable of human thoughts and feelings, the fact remains that this could happen someday. As Silver explains, "Modern biotechnology has moved such ambiguous beings from the realm of mythology to the realm of possibility. And this fact elicits the greatest challenge to western thought, which is that the existence of a strict line separating human beings from non-human beings may simply be a figment of our imagination."[35] The boundaries between what is considered right and wrong have also proved fluid to reflect the changing line between what is possible and what is impossible.

Baby Chimeras and Mouse Mommies

However, politicians and the scientific community alike are not content to leave these questions open to individual interpretation. In 2006 then-president George W. Bush asked Congress to pass legislation banning the creation of human-animal hybrids since, he believed, they devalued human life. Many share Bush's concern. However, no U.S. federal laws currently address these issues.

The National Academy of Sciences convened a committee in 2005 to provide voluntary ethical guidelines for chimera research. The committee, cochaired by biochemist Richard O. Hynes of the Massachusetts Institute of Technology, addressed two primary issues: engineering human cells into the germ lines of animals to create inheritable traits, and engineering brains that are partially human.

The first issue involves the production of human eggs and sperm by a nonhuman animal. If a male and female chimera with human eggs and sperm were to breed, they could theoretically produce a living human embryo. Most humans, the committee noted, would strongly object to the knowledge that their parents were mice or some other nonhuman mammal. To prevent this, the committee ruled that breeding chimeras is unethical. The rulings, however, have no regulatory power—they are merely recommendations.

The second issue targets research in which human cells are transferred into the brains of other animals, particularly primates, such as apes and chimpanzees. The committee also denounced

By using a process similar to in vitro fertilization, scientists believe it is possible to create a human-animal hybrid by injecting the sperm of an animal into the egg of a human.

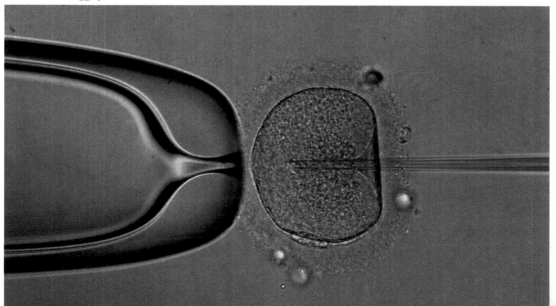

these experiments. Since humans and chimpanzees are close genetic cousins, the survival of such a creature is actually feasible. Richard Doerflinger of the U.S. Conference of Catholic Bishops expresses the concern of many when he says, "If something were half human and half animal, what would our moral responsibilities be? It might be immoral to kill such a creature [by experimenting on it]. It's wrong to create creatures whose moral stature we are perplexed about."[36]

Doerflinger is not alone in his discomfort. Biotechnology activist Jeremy Rifkin objects on other grounds. He believes that animals have the right to exist without human tampering. He favors the use of computer models rather than live animals to study disease systems. David Magnus, director of the Stanford Center for Biomedical Ethics at Stanford University, also expresses concern that chimeras will be used in ways that could be risky, problematic, or dangerous. He uses the possibility of a human born of mice parents as a good example of the possible consequences.

Other countries have been more proactive. Canada, for example, passed the Assisted Human Reproduction Act, which specifically bans chimeras. In Canada it is illegal to transfer a nonhuman cell into a human embryo. Canada also bans the transfer of human cells into nonhuman embryos. Weissman, who created the mice with partially human brains, opposes a similar ban in the United States. He explains, "Anybody who puts their own moral guidance in the way of this biomedical science, where they want to impose their will—not just be part of an argument—if that leads to a ban or moratorium . . . [it] is stopping research that would save human lives."[37]

However, like every other aspect of genetic engineering, the technology involved in the genetic engineering of humans moves quickly. Furthermore, it is not always clear from the outset just how a new science or technology will play out once it is released from the strictly controlled environment of the laboratory. Like the DNA that genetic engineering seeks to improve, genetic engineering itself interacts with the social, political, and cultural environment in ways that can be unexpected. Complex new ethical dilemmas arise even as society struggles to resolve the old ones.

EXTREME GENETIC ENGINEERING: THE FUTURE

Like a jigsaw puzzle, finding and fitting the first pieces of genetic engineering were the most difficult. Once the basic outline is complete, however, the remaining pieces tend to fall into place. Genetic engineering, however, is a puzzle that presents unique challenges. Each time another piece of this puzzle is solved, the puzzle evolves and becomes more complex.

Smells Like . . . Mint

Rapid advances in the understanding of how the genes work and parallel progress in the fields of engineering and technology have resulted in two fields of study that now capture a great deal of attention: bioengineering and biotechnology. Engineers focus on how things work and how to make them work efficiently. Bioengineers apply those concepts to living things. Biotechnology involves the use of technology to make or change products for specific purposes. Biotechnologists, for example, develop ways to treat waste, manufacture

Bioengineers focus on how living things work and how to make them work efficiently. Their understanding of how genes operate helps them to solve problems like creating pest-resistant varieties of corn and soy.

biological weapons, and make beer or cheese. They can even create pigs that glow in the dark.

Biotechnology is closely related to genetic engineering, since bioengineers apply the growing understanding of how genes work to solve some of the planet's most perplexing problems. Bioengineers are responsible for creating pest-resistant varieties of corn and soy and transferring genes between species to develop organs for transplant or ready sources of insulin.

At the Massachusetts Institute of Technology (MIT), graduate students in one bioengineering lab were tired of having to smell *E. coli*, a bacterium they were using in their experiments. *E. coli* emits the distinctive odor associated with feces. Their solution: They created minty fresh, wintergreen *E. coli* by combining the

What a Gem!

The International Genetically Engineered Machine Competition (iGEM) sponsored by the Massachusetts Institute of Technology is a worldwide event that addresses the question, "Can simple biological systems be built from standard, interchangeable parts and operated in living cells?" In order to answer this question, teams of participants—mostly college undergraduates—are supplied with standardized biological parts known as BioBricks. Their challenge: design and build genetic machines that perform useful functions. Students from universities around the world participate in the competition. In fact, half of the teams come from outside the United States. The interchangeable biological parts consist mostly of bacterial genes, such as *E. coli*, although some use plant, mammal, and stem cells. A team from MIT, for example, genetically programmed *E. Coli* to smell like mint while it was growing, then switch to the scent of banana to indicate it was done. The sweet-smelling bacteria might someday improve the odors from landfills, sewage treatment plants, and even armpits. An article in the *Boston Globe* explains: "The goal of the competition is to get young scientists to help spawn new industries in synthetic biology and make sure scientists worldwide are involved." The winner of the grand prize takes home the iGEM cup, a large aluminum BioBrick.

Tracy Jan, "Genetic 'Jamboree' Draws Innovators," *Boston Globe*, November 5, 2006. www.boston.com/news/education/higher/articles/2006/11/05/genetic_jamboree_draws_innovators.

wintergreen gene from petunia plants with *E. coli* bacteria. As a result of this genetic engineering feat, the *E. coli* in their lab then smelled like mint. Moreover, they engineered the bacteria further by inserting a biological trigger that changed the scent from mint to banana when the *E. coli* stopped growing. They could now engage in leisure activities within smelling distance of the lab while they waited for the olfactory signal to change from mint to banana.

Including the World

"If we have another huge industrial revolution, it's really important that it happens worldwide. We have to have people all over the world making materials and energy to meet their own needs." — Randy Rettberg, MIT research engineer who runs the iGEM contest.

Quoted in Tracy Jan, "Genetic 'Jamboree' Draws Innovators," *Boston Globe*, November 5, 2006. www.boston.com/news/education/higher/arti cles/2006/11/05/genetic_jamboree_draws_in novators.

Bioengineers regularly cross boundaries between life forms in their quest for novel solutions to vexing problems. However, until very recently their efforts were limited to genes that were already available. As the twenty-first century moves into its second decade, bioengineers are now learning to build genes from scratch to accomplish specific tasks. The ability to build new genes has given birth to a new field: synthetic biology. Synthetic biology, sometimes called "extreme genetic engineering" or "genetic engineering on steroids," raises questions about the very meaning of life itself. Is life just a machine made of parts that can be assembled and reassembled in various combinations? Synthetic biologists think so.

Genes Made to Order

Synthetic biology is built on the premise that the genes in all living things are composed of sequences of only four chemical bases: adenine (A), guanine (G), cytosine (C), and thymine (T). The genes of plants, animals, and bacteria vary only by the arrangements of these four chemical bases in the DNA, the twisted double-helix molecule that resides within the cells. Fifty years ago, scientists created the first tiny snippet of artificial DNA by artificially linking these four crucial chemicals.

However, not until 2008 did scientists report they had created the entire genome of a bacterium, which was ten times longer than any that had been previously synthesized. The *New York Times* called this a watershed event, meaning it would change the course of science. Once scientists become adept at synthesizing entire genomes, that knowledge will enable them to construct entirely new forms of life with specific functions. Andrew Pollack, *New York Times* science reporter, explains, "Synthetic biologists envision being able to design an organism on a

J. Craig Venter of Synthetic Genomics built the first completely artificial bacterium and is working to develop organisms that produce ethanol, hydrogen, and other alternative fuels to run vehicles.

computer, press the print button to have the necessary DNA made and then put that DNA into a cell to produce a custom-made creature."[38]

Many scientists hope that solutions to global problems that have so far defied science might lie in synthetic biology. J. Craig Venter, whose biotech company Synthetic Genomics in Rockville, Maryland, built the first completely artificial bacterium, is known to be working to develop organisms that produce ethanol, hydrogen, and other alternative fuels to run vehicles. These fuel-spewing organisms would provide an alternative source of fuel as well as enrich the company that wins the first patent on the technology. Some estimate the market for this future fuel could exceed $1 trillion. Other biotech companies hope to beat Venter in the race for this patent and have flooded the U.S. Patent and Trademark Office with patent requests, hoping to cash in on this quickly growing and promising technology.

The development of alternative fuel, however, is only one application that propels research in "synbio," as people in the field often call it. Jay D. Keasling at the University of California at Berkeley is developing synthetic DNA that will allow genes from the wormwood tree and yeast to work together within *E. coli* bacteria to produce a steady source of artemisinin, a drug used to treat malaria. Malaria is a leading cause of death and illness worldwide.

Scientists at the California Institute of Technology in Pasadena, California, are building artificial biological circuits that can be inserted in the body's cells to guard against cancer. Like miniature early warning systems, these circuits trigger automatic self-destruction in cells that develop cancer.

Genes to Go: Cheap and Easy

Though many scientists and entrepreneurs foresee great promise in synthetic biology, the field is still quite new. For the time being, most synthetic biology remains only partly synthetic, relying on natural organisms to do the bulk of the genetic work. It has been described as "a cut and paste operation, like writing a phrase by snipping the necessary words out of magazines and gluing them together in the proper order."[39]

GENETICALLY ENGINEERING A HOUSE

"'Grow a house' is on the to-do list of the MIT [Massachusetts Institute of Technology] Synthetic Biology Working Group, presumably meaning that an acorn might be reprogrammed to generate walls, oak floors, and a roof instead of the usual trunk and branches." —Nicholas Wade, science writer and editor.

Nicholas Wade, "Genetic Engineers Who Don't Just Tinker," *New York Times*, July 8, 2007. www.nytimes.com/2007/07/08/weekinreview/08wade.html?_r=1&ref=science&oref=slogin.

Tom Knight, an MIT researcher, has compared the current state of synthetic biology to mechanical engineering in the mid-1800s. At that time the United States began to adopt standardized sizes for nuts and bolts, a development that allowed the construction of complex machines from simple interchangeable parts. Knight and his colleagues have begun the process of developing interchangeable genetic units they call BioBricks, which can be popped into cells like tiny Legos. As they become more common, they also become less expensive. So-called "biofabs," or biological fabrication machines, can produce made-to-order genes for less than $1 per A-T or G-C base pair. Scientists need only specify the desired genetic sequence, place an order over the Internet, and await delivery of the finished gene within a week or so.

It May Be Convenient, but Is It Safe?

Not everyone expresses unconditional enthusiasm about the ability to place orders for life like so much take-out food, however. Many voice concern that DNA synthesis might be used in sinister ways. Some fear the possibility of deadly organisms contaminating the environment in purposeful acts of bioterrorism.

In 2002 scientists at Stony Brook University in New York State announced they had synthesized the poliovirus using information that is readily available. In fact, they ordered the necessary base pairs over the Internet. In England, a reporter for the *Guardian*, a British newspaper, placed an order for a synthetic fragment of smallpox DNA and had it delivered to his home. Smallpox is a highly contagious virus that disappeared almost

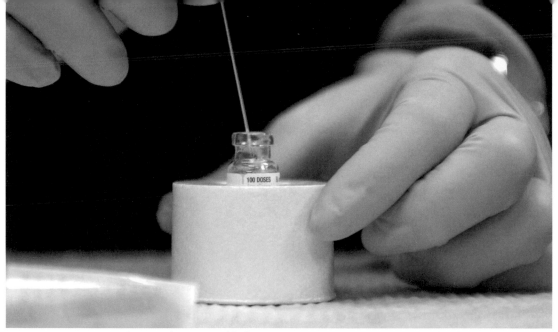

DNA synthesis makes it possible for scientists to create smallpox in a lab. The Centers for Disease Control and Prevention reports that it has enough of the vaccine (pictured here) to vaccinate everybody in the United States should an epidemic occur.

entirely more than thirty years ago. Scientists have also re-created the virus responsible for the deadly flu epidemic that killed more than 50 million people worldwide in 1918 and 1919.

In 2005 the U.S. Department of Health and Human Services published the full genome of that virus on the Internet as part of an article that detailed how the virus had evolved from simple bird flu to a deadly human epidemic. Two science writers, Ray Kurzweil and Bill Joy, in an editorial titled "Recipe for Destruction," expressed outrage that such potentially dangerous information was so easily accessible: "The genome is essentially the design of a weapon of mass destruction. No responsible scientist would advocate publishing precise designs for an atomic bomb, and in two ways revealing the sequence for the flu virus is even more dangerous. We should treat the genetic sequences of pathological biological viruses with no less care than designs for nuclear weapons."[40] They point out, in fact, that it would be easier to create a synthetic flu virus than to build a bomb from published information. And, they add, the virus could be far more destructive. While an atom bomb dropped on an American city could kill as many as a million people, the release of a deadly biological virus could kill tens of millions. The two writers emphasize the need for strict limits on availability of this type of information.

Others are not content to leave the responsibility for policing production of synthetic organisms to self-regulation by the synbio industry. One reason for their skepticism about the wisdom of self-regulation is the potential for profit. Some of the most important researchers in the field also stand to reap huge profits if their research is successful.

Keasling from the University of California at Berkeley is a cofounder of Amyris Biotechnologies, which is developing the malaria drug. He and Drew Endy, an MIT researcher, are involved in Codon Devices, a company in Cambridge, Massachusetts, that is developing a less expensive technique to synthesize DNA. Venter established the company Synthetic Genomics to work on the development of bacteria for biofuel production. He is also the founder and CEO of the Venter Institute, a company that applied for a patent on the world's first completely synthetic living organism, aptly named Synthia. Jim Thomas, a spokesman for ETC, a public watchdog group that monitors the sociological and environmental effects of new technology, responded to Venter's announcement by contrasting it with the creation of Dolly, the cloned sheep: "Synthia may not be as cuddly as a cloned lamb, but we believe this is a much bigger deal. These monopoly claims signal the stake of a high-stakes commercial race to synthesize and privatize synthetic life forms."[41] The ETC group appealed to Venter—who some compare to Microsoft's successful founder Bill Gates—to withdraw the patent application until the public has the chance to debate its implications fully.

The Health and Human Services Department established the National Science Advisory Board for Biosecurity in 2005 to address these potential conflicts of interest. It advises researchers who work with potentially dangerous biological materials. That board, in turn, set up a committee to deal specifically with synthetic genomes. David A. Reiman, an associate professor of medicine at Stanford University and chairman of that committee, agreed that synthetic biology holds both promises and perils. He said, "We fully recognize the inherent beneficial and very positive attributes of all of this work and don't want to stifle it or curtail it or constrain it for no substantive reason."[42]

However, everyone, including Reiman, acknowledges that the potential dangers go beyond the unlikely chance that someone will create deadly organisms and create intentional public health havoc. The fact remains that synthetic genes are composed of hundreds of thousands of A-T and G-C base pairs. People input the information into computers and wait for machines to print out the finished DNA sequences. Just as the spell-check and grammar-check features on word processors depend on humans to program correct spelling and grammar into computers, biofabs depend on humans, too. Humans must input the DNA sequences, and humans develop the machines that print them out. Mistakes are common. In fact, to minimize error, companies often make a series of shorter sequences and then splice them together.

SPACE CADETS

"In short, bioengineers are the space cadets of engineering, going boldly where no engineers have gone before, and they seem to be having a remarkably good time, to a degree that worries some traditional biologists and a few cranky journalists." —Robert Krulwich, science correspondent for National Public Radio.

Robert Krulwich, "Minty *E.Coli* and Other Bioengineering Feats," National Public Radio, March 14, 2008. www.npr.org/templates/story/story.php?storyId=90014997.

Another concern is that even if mistakes are eliminated entirely, living organisms—even synthetic ones—are still unpredictable. When they leave the controlled world of the laboratory, they interact with the environment in ways that can be unexpected. The fear exists, even among the researchers most closely involved with the technology, that synthetic genes might run amok and cause unforeseen public health disasters.

Who Needs DNA Anyway?

Biosafety is one force that motivates some researchers to eliminate DNA from the mix altogether. Most of the work in synthetic biology—and in genetic engineering in general—involves duplicating or somehow tweaking the DNA molecule. One way or

Like a droplet of oil in water, Steen Rasmussen's cell parts were designed to keep water out of the cell.

another, DNA is the central focus. One research team, led by Steen Rasmussen, a theoretical physicist at the Los Alamos National Research Laboratory in New Mexico, is going in a different direction. Rather than attempting to create synthetic versions of known cell parts, this team is designing brand-new parts to fulfill the cell's essential functions.

Rasmussen and his team believe that every cell needs three things: a metabolism that produces its energy, a molecule like DNA that stores information, and a membrane that holds everything together. Natural cells rely on an oily membrane to keep water inside the cell. Rasmussen's cell—which he has dubbed the Bug—is basically a droplet of oil, which keeps water out of the cell. Also, the basic structure of the Bug's double-helix molecule that stores its information differs from that of DNA. Howard Packer, who works with Rasmussen, explains that this structural difference serves as an extra measure of biosafety protection. In the event the Bug escapes, this structural difference ensures that the two systems cannot mix, which could have unintended consequences.

A company called ProtoLife was founded by Rasmussen and Packard in Venice, Italy, to continue their research and eventually market the Bug and its components. While right now they concede their research lags behind that of mainstream synthetic biology, they believe the Bug is promising. Rasmussen explains why he believes the Bug will ultimately prevail: "Right now, the state of the art for synthetic biology is a hodgepodge of techniques, which are, from a scientific and engineering perspective, groping."[43] He expresses confidence that ProtoLife will produce a functioning cell in the near future. He also believes that building a cell by creating its essential ingredients will lead to a better understanding of living and nonliving systems in general.

Expanding the Genetic Code

While some researchers focus on replicating the structure and function of DNA, others see no reason that every life form in the universe is necessarily limited to combinations of A, G, C, and T. *Extreme Genetic Engineering*, a report by the ETC Group, describes the work of Steven Benner, a pioneer in synthetic biology and founder of the Westheimer Institute for Science and Technology: "His [Benner's] argument is simple: there is no reason the limited set of molecules in DNA should be the only form of life that has arisen in the universe and we need models of what other kind of life could be out there. He sees artificial genetics as a way to explore basic questions, such as how life got started on earth, how it evolves and even what forms it may take elsewhere in the universe."[44] Benner and his team created a molecule that functions like DNA but contains two artificial bases in addition to the four that occur in nature. Later, they expanded that number to twelve. Benner calls his system of bases AEGIS (An Expanded Genetic Information System) and has commercially licensed the system to a private biotech company.

Other scientists have built on Benner's work to develop other artificial genetic systems. A Stanford University chemist, for example, has redesigned the A-T base pair to be larger, glow in the dark, and withstand high temperatures without breaking down. Benner and others believe that in the near future they will successfully create artificial life that can learn, reproduce, evolve, and respond to the environment.

Biohacking: A New Hobby for Do-It-Yourselfers

While professional scientists meddle with the building blocks of life, a group of serious amateurs participate in DIYbio—short for do-it-yourself biology. Their goal is to bring biology into the hands of hobbyists. Groups of DIYbiologists meet to extract DNA

Scientists and researchers at Massachusetts Institute of Technology have made several contributions to the field of synthetic biology.

and perform DNA experiments using common household products and tools. While bringing this science into the public realm has some benefits, it also worries some scientists. Although the term *biohacking* sounds illegal, serious scientists use it to refer to the work of amateurs devoted to arranging cells and genes in creative ways. An article in the *Tech*, MIT's campus newspaper, spells out how synthetic biology eases the efforts of biohackers: "The dream . . . is that biology novices could browse a catalog of ready-made biological parts and use them to create customized organisms."[45] However, just as computer hackers can create deadly computer viruses, so biohackers might create deadly microbes.

Tom Knight, a senior researcher at MIT, cofounded a synthetic biology company he named Gingko BioWorks. He sees value in the ingenuity of do-it-yourself biologists. In fact, he and a group of synthetic biologists at MIT identify themselves as biohackers. However, Knight also voices reservations about the safety of making biological information so readily accessible. He says, "I think if the safety issues can be addressed, there is a big opportunity. It's a huge issue; how do you regulate so [people] don't cause havoc."[46] According to the *Tech*, Gingko acknowledged the excitement of amateur scientists by publishing a comic book style guide to biohacking. Each frame demonstrates a small bioengineering experiment. The company compares backyard genetic engineering to the early days of computer technology when young entrepreneurs such as Bill Gates of Microsoft launched companies in their basements and garages.

Evolution on Overdrive

As scientists become more adept at engineering and synthesizing the microscopic components of life—whether synthetic or natural—the issues surrounding these accomplishments loom large. Questions about who should profit and how genetic engineering should be controlled have yet to be resolved. Yet even as entire industries focus their sights on these extreme versions of genetic engineering, an issue of massive proportions troubles many scientists and members of the public. Some envision a foreboding future when and if genetic engineering—especially the genetic engineering of humans—becomes commonplace.

DIVERSITY WITHOUT RESTRAINT

"It is difficult to imagine several human species coexisting peacefully on this small and crowded planet. To allow the diversification of human genomes and lifestyles on this planet to continue without restraint is a recipe for disaster." —Freeman J. Dyson, physicist, Institute for Advanced Study, Princeton University.

Freeman J. Dyson, *The Sun, the Genome, and the Internet.* New York: Oxford University Press, 1999, p. 113.

Some people, including Silver at Princeton University, believe humans could be headed toward a world inhabited by two very different human species. In his book *Challenging Nature*, Silver paints a picture of what the future might hold if genetic engineering proceeds unchecked. He describes two human species, which he calls "naturals" and "enhanced," that could result. Naturals will depend on old-fashioned genetic luck. Enhanced humans will have advantages endowed by genes either selected or engineered to provide superior intelligence, talents, looks, and other traits. Each successive generation will have the opportunity to enhance even further the genetic fortunes of their children. Genetic advantages will pass from one generation to another. Eventually, the two groups will differ so greatly they will have evolved into different species.

When Charles Darwin proposed his theory of evolution in the 1850s, he explained how species evolve to adapt to challenges in the environment.

THE ORIGIN OF SPECIES

BY MEANS OF NATURAL SELECTION,

OR THE

PRESERVATION OF FAVOURED RACES IN THE STRUGGLE FOR LIFE.

By CHARLES DARWIN, M.A.,

FELLOW OF THE ROYAL, GEOLOGICAL, LINNÆAN, ETC., SOCIETIES;
AUTHOR OF 'JOURNAL OF RESEARCHES DURING H. M. S. BEAGLE'S VOYAGE
ROUND THE WORLD.'

LONDON:
JOHN MURRAY, ALBEMARLE STREET.
1859.

Silver is particularly troubled by how that will play out in society. When he was interviewed by the British Broadcasting Company, he told reporters:

> I don't think those people [the naturals and the enhanced] would be able to interact very well and so they will stay apart from each other socially, and ultimately they won't be able to breed with each other. I think it's going to be a disaster because one group of people who is a different species to the other group of people will no longer have the desire or need to treat that second group with dignity and respect.[47]

Money, of course, will be the deciding factor, according to Silver. People with ample resources will have genetic choices. Poor people will not.

This scenario is not as far-fetched as it once may have seemed. When Charles Darwin proposed his theory of evolution in the 1850s, he explained how species evolve to adapt to challenges in the environment. Some modern biologists believe that genetic engineering signals the end of Darwinian evolution. Humans are now on the brink of directing evolution on their own terms.

No longer will it be necessary to wait thousands of years for small changes to become apparent. Farmers already grow food crops genetically engineered to resist pests or provide more nutrition. Scientists raise livestock genetically engineered to produce organs for human transplant. A race is on to perfect a way to bypass animals altogether and cultivate meat in vats from genetically engineered cells. Manufacturers weave fiber as strong as steel from the genetically engineered milk of goats.

This is not science fiction. This is real science. And most of these accomplishments have occurred within the last ten years. In the meantime, the primary question itself has evolved along with the science. No longer is the question whether or not humans are able to challenge nature in such profound ways. Instead, the question has become: Just how far will it go?

Introduction: A Scientific Revolution

1. Robert Krulwich, "Minty *E. Coli* and Other Bioengineering Feats," *Morning Edition*, National Public Radio, April 29, 2008. www.npr.org/templates/story/story.php?storyId=90014 997.

Chapter 1: Pharming: The Disease or the Cure?

2. Freeman J. Dyson, *The Sun, The Genome, and the Internet*. New York: Oxford University Press, 1999, p. 17.

3. Elizabeth Svoboda, "Pharm Animals Crank Out Drugs," Wired, February 14, 2007. www.wired.com/medtech/health/news/2007/02/72708.

4. Svoboda, "Pharm Animals Crank Out Drugs."

5. Quoted in Mark Henderson, "Mutant Monkeys Bred to Contract Brain Disorder," *London Times*, May 19, 2008. www.timesonline.co.uk/tol/news/uk/science/article3958803.ece.

6. mdr, "When Pigs Glow," Science Buzz, January 10, 2008. www.smm.org/buzz/blog/when_pigs_glow.

7. Quoted in The Organic and Non-GMO Report, "Genetic Engineering of Food Crops to Produce Drugs Raises Concern," September 2002. www.non-gmoreport.com/Genetic_engineering.php.

8. Quoted in Environment News Service, "Farmers Worry About Genetically Altered Rice Approval," May 21, 2007. www.ens-newswire.com/ens/may2007/2007-05-21-09.asp.

9. Quoted in Margot Roosevelt, "Cures on the Cob," *Time*, May 19, 2003. www.time.com/time/magazine/article/0,9171,4528 04-1,00.html.

10. Alla Katsnelson, "Fear of Pharming," *Scientific American*, September 20, 2004. www.sciam.com/article.cfm?id=fear-of-pharming.

11. Quoted in Linda Bren, "Genetic Engineering: The Future of Foods?" U.S. Food and Drug Administration, 2003. www.fda .gov/fdac/features/2003/603_food.html.

Chapter 2: Genetically Engineered Foods: Whose Appetite Do They Satisfy?

12. Public Issues Education Project: Genetically Engineered Organisms, "Fish-Gene Strawberries and Tomatoes," Cornell University. www.geo-pie.cornell.edu/media/fishberries.html.

13. Elena Conis, "Biotech Foods Are Hard to Swallow," *Los Angeles Times*, October 22, 2007. http://ucbiotech.org/news/ar ticles/102207.pdf.

14. Quoted in Andrew Pollack, "Without U.S. Rules, U.S. Food Lacks Investors," *New York Times*, July 30, 2007. www.ny times.com/2007/07/30/washington/30animal.html?page wanted=1&sq=Aqua%20Bounty%20salmon&st=cse&scp=2.

15. Quoted in Ben Macintyre, "Will the Petri Dish Put Daisy Out to Grass?" Times Online, January 13, 2007. http://business.timeson line.co.uk/tol/business/markets/europe/article12923 46.ece.

16. Quoted in Jim Kling, "Future Feast," New Harvest, December 2006. www.new-harvest.org/article12012006.htm.

17. Pew Initiative on Food and Biotechnology, "Three Years Later: Genetically Engineered Corn and the Monarch Butterfly Controversy," 2002, p. 3. www.pewtrusts.org/uploadedFiles/www pewtrustsorg/Reports/Food_and_Biotechnology/vf_biotech_ monarch.pdf.

18. Quoted in Andrew Pollack, "In Lean Times, Biotech Grains Are Less Taboo," *New York Times*, April 21, 2008, p. A16.

19. Freeman J. Dyson, "Our Biotech Future," *New York Review of Books*, July 19, 2007. www.nybooks.com/articles/20370.

Chapter 3: From Fabric to Fuel

20. Michael Fumento, "Protein Power," *American Outlook*, Fall 2002. www.fumento.com/biotech/protein.html.

21. Quoted in Lawrence Osborne, "Got Silk?" *New York Times Magazine*, June 16, 2002, p. 2. http://query.nytimes.com/gst/ fullpage.html?res=9C05E7DD113DF935A25755C0A9649C 8B63&sec=&spon=&&scp=1&sq=BioSteel&st=cse.

22. Quoted in Marilyn Berlin Snell, "Fashion Statement," Profile, *Sierra Magazine*, January/February 2005. www.sierraclub.org/sierra/200501/hamnett2.asp.

23. Yvon Chouinard, "What Does a Clothing Company Know About Genetic Engineering?" *Patagonia*, Winter 2002. www.patagonia.com/web/eu/patagonia.go?assetid=9134.

24. Wenjian Wang, Sankha Bhowmick, Debra Ellis, Steven Warner, and Alex Fowler, "Loading of Genetically Engineered Bacteria into Hollow Milkweed Fibers," Summer Bioengineering Conference, Tulane University, 2003. www.tulane.edu/~sbc2003/pdfdocs/1149.PDF.

25. Andrew Pollack, "Redesigning Crops to Harvest Fuel," *New York Times*, September 8, 2006. www.nytimes.com/2006/09/08/business/08crop.html?fta=y.

26. Quoted in Michael Kanellos, "Biodiesel Venture Combines Refining, Genetic Engineering," CNET News.com, November 19, 2007. http://news.cnet.com/Biodiesel-venture-com bines-re fining,-genetic-engineering/2100-13844_3-6219431 .html.

27. Dyson, "Our Biotech Future."

Chapter 4: Designer Babies

28. Michael D. Lemonick, "Designer Babies," *Time*, January 11, 1999, p. 64.

29. Mike Polyakov, "The Ethics of Designer Children," Institute for Ethics and Emerging Technologies, April 10, 2008. http://ieet.org/index.php/IEET/more/polyakov20080410.

30. Polyakov, "The Ethics of Designer Children."

31. Carl T. Hall, "The Modified Man," Center for Genetics and Society, July 3, 2008.

32. Scott LaFee, "The Race Against Gene Doping," *San Diego Union-Tribune*, July 27, 2008, p. A12.

33. Nicholas D. Kristof, "Where Is Thy Sting?" *New York Times*, August 12, 2003. http://query.nytimes.com/gst/fullpage.html?res=9404EEDC1131F931A2575BC0A9659C8B63&n=Top/Opinion/Editorials%20and%20Op-Ed/Op-Ed/Columnists/Nicholas%20D%20Kristof&scp=1&sq=Kristoff%20Where%20is%20Thy%20Sting?&st=cse.

34. Stuart Newman, "Extended Interview: Stuart Newman," PBS

Online NewsHour, July 2005. www.pbs.org/newshour/bb/
science/july-dec05/chimeras_newman-ext.html.

35. Lee Silver, "Human-Animal Chimeras: From Mythology to
Biotechnology," *Scientific Blogging*, February 15, 2007.

36. Quoted in Nicholas Wade, "Chimeras on the Horizon but
Don't Expect Centaurs," *New York Times*, May 3, 2003. www
.nytimes.com/2005/05/03/science/03chim.html?page
wanted=1&_r=1&oref=slogin.

37. Quoted in Maryann Mott, "Animal-Human Hybrids Spark
Controversy," *National Geographic News*, January 25, 2005.
http://news.nationalgeographic.com/news/2005/01/
0125_050125_chimeras.html.

Chapter 5: Extreme Genetic Engineering: The Future

38. Andrew Pollack, "Researchers Take Step Toward Synthetic
Life," *New York Times*, January 25, 2008, p. A17. www.nytimes
.com/2008/01/25/science/25genome.html.

39. Quoted in Andrew Pollack, "How Do You Like Your Genes?
Biofabs Take Orders," *New York Times*, September 12, 2007.
www.nytimes.com/2007/09/12/technology/techspecial/12gene
.html.

40. Ray Kurzweil and Bill Joy, "Recipe for Destruction," *New York
Times*, October 17, 2005. www.nytimes.com/2005/10/17/
opinion/17kurzweiljoy.html?scp=1&sq=recipe%20for%20de
struction&st=cse.

41. Quoted in ETC Group, "Goodbye Dolly, Hello Synthia," news
release, June 7, 2007. www.etcgroup.org/en/materials/publi
cations.html?pub_id=631.

42. Quoted in Andrew Pollack, "Custom-Made Microbes, at Your
Service," *New York Times*, January 17, 2006. http://query.ny
times.com/gst/fullpage.html?sec=health&res=9B03E6D
A143FF934A25752C0A9609C8B63.

43. Quoted in ETC Group, *Extreme Genetic Engineering: An Introduction to Synthetic Biology*, report, January 2007, p. 19.

44. ETC Group, *Extreme Genetic Engineering*, p. 21.

45. Carolyn Y. Johnson, "As Synthetic Biology Becomes Afford-
able, Amateur Labs Thrive," *Tech*, September 16, 2008. http://
tech.mit.edu/V128/N39/biohack.html.

46. Quoted in Johnson, "As Synthetic Biology Becomes Afford-able, Amateur Labs Thrive."

47. Quoted in *Frontpage*, "Back to the Future," BBC News, December 1999. http://news.bbc.co.uk/hi/english/static/special_report/1999/12/99/back_to_the_future/lee_silver.stm.

DISCUSSION QUESTIONS

Chapter 1: Pharming: The Disease or the Cure?

1. In what ways has genetic engineering changed the traditional use of medicinal plants?
2. How do both humans and biotechnology companies benefit from pharmaceuticals developed by genetic engineering?
3. According to the author, why would scientists deliberately cause diseases in animals?
4. How does genetically engineering jellyfish genes into pigs and other animals benefit scientific research?
5. Why do critics of genetic engineering so often mention the Starlink scandal?

Chapter 2: Genetically Engineered Foods: Whose Appetite Do They Satisfy?

1. Describe the main conflict between proponents and critics of Roundup Ready soy and *Bt* corn.
2. In what ways might producing rainbow trout with an extra set of chromosomes benefit the fishing industry? Explain how this feature might also protect wild trout.
3. Explain why meat grown in a vat is so controversial, even among animal lovers.
4. How has the organic-food movement benefited from genetically engineered foods?
5. According to the author, what are some situations that tend to decrease resistance to genetically engineered foods?

Chapter 3: From Fabric to Fuel

1. Explain how genetic engineering has helped create a lightweight, flexible fabric that could have military applications. What do scientists still not understand about how a spider spins its web?

2. Explain why the fashion industry has embraced organic cotton.
3. According to the author, why might fuel from genetically engineered camelina prove more acceptable than fuel from corn?

Chapter 4: Designer Babies

1. According to the author, how does the term "designer babies" offer a clue to public opinion about the genetic engineering of children?
2. In what ways does modern genetic engineering differ from eugenics, as it was practiced in the nineteenth and twentieth centuries?
3. Why are some scientists concerned about the method used in gene therapy to carry replacement genes into the cells?
4. Explain the arguments both for and against gene doping. Why is it so difficult to detect?
5. Why might people object to genetic engineering that results in organisms that have obvious human features, while they do not object to organisms that do not appear human?

Chapter 5: Extreme Genetic Engineering: The Future

1. Why does synthetic biology lead people to question the meaning of life itself?
2. How might the ability to order genes online prove dangerous?
3. How does Steen Rasmussen's "Bug" differ from natural cells?
4. Explain Lee Silver's concerns about the development of two distinct human species.

Biotechnology Industry Organization (BIO)
1201 Maryland Ave. SW, Ste. 900
Washington, DC 20024
phone: (202) 962-9200
fax: (202) 488-6301
e-mail: info@bio.org

BIO is the world's largest biotechnology organization. It advocates the research, development, and commercial distribution of products that result from genetic engineering.

Center for Genetics and Society
436 Fourteenth St., Ste. 700
Oakland, CA 94612
phone: (510) 625-0819
fax: (510) 625-0874
e-mail: info@geneticsandsociety.org

This nonprofit information and public affairs organization encourages responsible use and effective societal governance of the new human genetic and reproductive technologies. It supports some medical applications and opposes others that threaten to divide human society.

Council for Responsible Genetics
5 Upland Rd., Ste. 3
Cambridge, MA 02140
phone: (617) 868-0870
fax: (617) 491-5344
e-mail: crg@gene-watch.org

This nonprofit organization fosters public debate about the social, ethical, and environmental impacts of genetic technology.

Greenpeace USA
702 H St. NW, Ste. 300
Washington, DC 20001
phone: (202) 462-1177
e-mail: www.greenpeace.org/usa

Greenpeace lobbies to limit or ban products that are the result of genetic engineering. Greenpeace has offices worldwide.

Northwest Resistance Against Genetic Engineering (NW Rage)
PO Box 15289
Portland, OR 97293
phone: (503) 239-6841
e-mail: info@nwrage.org

NW Rage is a nonviolent, grassroots organization dedicated to promoting the responsible, sustainable, and just use of agriculture and science. It advocates the ban of genetic engineering and patents on life. It focuses on education, community building, advocacy, and action.

Organic Consumer Association (OCA)
6771 S. Silver Hill Dr.
Finland, MN 55603
phone: (218) 226-4164
fax: (218) 353-7652
e-mail: www.organicconsumers.org

The OCA is an online, grassroots public interest organization that deals with food safety, industrial agriculture, and genetic engineering. Its focus is promoting the views and interests of consumers of organic products.

Union of Concerned Scientists (UCS)
National Headquarters
2 Brattle Sq.
Cambridge, MA 02238-9105
phone: (617) 547-5552
fax: (617) 864-9405
e-mail: www.ucsusa.org

This science-based nonprofit organization working for a healthy environment and a safer world began as a collaboration of students and faculty members at MIT. UCS combines independent scientific research and citizen action to promote responsible government and corporate policies for cleaner and healthier air, energy, food, and transportation.

Books

John Avise, *The Hope, Hype, and Reality of Genetic Engineering: Remarkable Stories from Agriculture, Industry, Medicine, and the Environment.* New York: Oxford University Press, 2004. Written at a slightly advanced level, this book presents a clear overview of many of the more remarkable accomplishments of genetic engineering.

Ron Fridell, *Cool Science: Genetic Engineering.* Minneapolis: Lerner, 2005. An overview of how genetic engineering is used to invent plants, improve animals, and engineer people.

Lauri S. Friedman, ed., *Opposing Viewpoints: Genetically Modified Foods.* Farmington Hills, MI: Greenhaven, 2008. Examines many of the arguments of both critics and proponents of genetically modified foods, including: Are they safe? Should they be labeled? Will they alleviate world hunger? What is their effect on the environment?

Louise I. Gerdes, ed., *Opposing Viewpoints: Genetic Engineering.* Farmington Hills, MI: Greenhaven, 2004. Presents arguments by experts both in support of and opposed to genetic engineering.

Periodicals

David Bjerklie, "Trouble on the Table," *Time for Kids,* March 10, 2000. www.timeforkids.com/TFK/kids/wr/article/0,28391,491 09,00.html. Examines the growing prevalence of genetically engineering foods—both their benefits and potential dangers.

Dan Charles, "Genetically Engineering the Sweet Stuff," *All Things Considered,* NPR, February 14, 2008. www.npr.org/templates /story/story.php?storyId=18817571. Available in both recorded and print versions, this 2008 NPR story explains the struggle to gain USDA approval for Roundup Ready sugar beets, which the American Crystal Company hopes to process into table sugar.

Scott LaFee, "Shining Examples," Quest, *San Diego Union-Tribune*, October 16, 2008. A collection of color photographs and a description of some of the many organisms created by genetically engineering the jellyfish gene for fluorescent protein into the genomes of other animals.

Andrew Pollack, "Without U.S. Rules, Biotech Food Lacks Investors," *New York Times*, July 31, 2007. www.nytimes.com/ learning/ teachers/featured_articles/20070731tuesday.html. Explores the concerns about and benefits of genetically engineered foods.

———, "Dawn of Low-Price Mapping Could Broaden DNA Uses," *New York Times*, October 7, 2008. www.nytimes.com /learning/teachers/featured_articles/20081007tuesday.html. This article examines the rapid decrease in the cost of mapping an individual's genetic blueprint. As the price falls, more people are likely to discover what their future may hold.

D.J. Siegelbaum, "In Search of a Test-Tube Hamburger," *Time*, April 23, 2008. www.time.com/time/health/article/0,8599,17 34630,00.html. A discussion of the process of and the controversies surrounding PETA's offer of a $1 million prize for the first practical test-tube meat produced by 2012.

Web Sites

Adventures in Synthetic Biology (www.nature.com/nature/ comics/syntheticbiologycomic/index.html). This twelve-frame comic strip by Drew Endy and the MIT Synthetic Biology Working Group illustrates some of the concepts involved in programming DNA and genetic engineering. It is high level and visually appealing.

Farming with Borrowed Genes (www.nytimes.com/imagepages /2007/07/30/washington/20070730_biotech_graphic.html). A Web site from the *New York Times* Learning Network that includes images of animals being considered by the FDA for approval, including fast-growing salmon, omega-3-enriched pigs, and infection-resistant cows.

Human's Playground: Genetic Engineering (http://library.think quest.org/04apr/00774/en/index.html). Provides a video introduction and complete guide to the history, science, and issues involved in genetic engineering. Each section includes a bibliography and guide to video resources.

New Harvest (www.new-harvest.org/default.php). The mission of New Harvest is to advance research into meat substitutes. The Web site includes links to articles about cultured meat substitutes.

Northwest Resistance Against Genetic Engineering (www .Nwrage.org). The motto of this Web site is "Resistance Is Fertile!" It includes a complete list of resources, articles, and organizations that lobby against genetic engineering.

The Pinky Show Presents: Islands at Risk: Genetic Engineering in Hawaii (www.mefeedia.com/entry/pinky-presents-islands-at-risk-genetic-engineering-in-hawaii/6599565). This thirty-minute documentary was made in 2006 by Na Maka o ka Aina for Earthjustice, a nonprofit public interest law firm. It clearly explains the issues raised by genetic engineering but with an obvious critical bias, pointing out the many risks to humans, animals, and the environment.

Science Video Resources: "Genetic Engineering: Glowing Pigs and Fish" (http://sciencevideos.wordpress.com/2007/ 11/12/genetic-engineering-glowing-pigs-and-fish/). This startling five-minute glance at pigs and fish that have been genetically engineered to glow in the dark points out how this feature would be an evolutionary disadvantage to wildlife, functioning as a neon sign that says, "Eat me!" The same feature might, however, help monitor transplanted organs.

Video

Discovery Channel School, *Designer Babies.* http://discovery school.com/lessonplans/programs/geneticengineering/q.html. A discussion for students about the technological and ethical issues that arise as parents gain the ability to choose a child's gender, size, hair color, and intelligence as well as the option to have unborn children screened for diseases and birth defects. Includes thoughtful discussion questions for the classroom.

Podcast

WNYC, "(So Called) Life," *Radiolab*, March 14, 2008. www.wnyc
.org/shows/radiolab/episodes/2008/03/14. This radio documentary is devoted to synthetic biology and the connection
between biology and engineering. Very entertaining. Includes
the song "March of the Bioengineers."

INDEX

PICTURE CREDITS

Cover photo: Image copyright Sebastian Kaulitzki, 2009. Used under license from Shutterstock.com

Animals Animals © Breck P. Kent, 41

AP Images, 9, 13, 18, 21, 25, 38, 56, 62, 69, 80, 83

© Roger Bamber/Alamy, 35

© CC Studio/Science Photo Library, Photo Researchers, Inc., 75

© Corbis, 64

© Cut and Deal Ltd./Alamy, 67

Jay Directo/AFP/Getty Images, 44

© David Fleetham/Alamy, 71

© Jeff Greenberg/Alamy, 31

© David Howells/Corbis, 54

© Della Huff/Alamy, 88

© Wolfang Kaehler/Corbis, 47

© mediacolor's/Alamy, 49

Scott Olson/Getty Images, 51

© Phototake, Inc./Alamy, 16, 29, 65

Special Collections Library, University of Michigan, 90

© Stock Connection Blue/Alamy, 77

© A.T. Willett/Alamy, 86

ABOUT THE AUTHOR

After spending many years teaching young students, Tina Kafka now devotes her teaching to adults who are working to earn their GEDs (general equivalency diplomas) and go to college. She enjoys researching strange and curious topics.